MW00878406

The Quest for Christmas
Examining the Evidence for Belief

The Quest for Christmas
Examining the Evidence for Belief

Kyle Davison Bair

First Edition: December 2021

ISBN: 9798788087443

Printed in the United States of America

Scripture quotations marked NIV are from The Holy Bible, New International Version. Copyright © 1973, 1978, 1984, International Bible Society.

Scripture quotations marked ESV are from The Holy Bible, English Standard Version® (ESV®). Copyright © 2001 by Crossway, a publishing ministry of Good News Publishers.

Scripture quotations marked CJB are from The Complete Jewish Bible® Copyright ® 1998 by David H. Stern.

Scripture quotations marked NLT are from The Holy Bible, New Living Translation. Copyright ® 1996, 2004, 2015 by Tyndale House Foundation.

Scripture quotations marked MSG are from The Message: The Bible in Contemporary Language. Copyright ®2002 by Eugene H. Peterson.

Scripture quotations marked JC:TGL are from Jesus Christ: The Greatest Life: A Unique Blending of the Four Gospels. Compiled and translated by Johnston M. Cheney and Stanley Ellisen. Copyright ©1999 by R.A. Meltebeke and S. Meltebeke.

All boldface, italics, or underling added to Scripture quotations is the author's addition.

Cover photo by Sincerely Media on Unsplash Used under the Unsplash License.

This book is dedicated to the curious –
to those who continually ask "why," who search out the
evidence, who cannot rest until they know the truth that
is fully worthy of belief.

May you keep asking, seeking, searching – and finding.

Table of Contents

The Prophecy

The Meaning

Acknowledgement

I owe a great debt of gratitude to all the beta readers on my blog at pastorkyle.substack.com. The feedback provided has been exceptional, helping craft these chapters into the best book they can be.

I also owe a great debt to my family – to Cassie, Ira, Talis, and especially Ezra, who allowed me to write while holding him for hours on end:

Introduction: Launching the Quest for Christmas

What should we believe about Christmas?

We all want to believe *something* around Christmas time. Endless movies, songs, and books search for the true meaning of Christmas. Something intrinsic to the Christmas season prompts us to search for meaning and purpose unlike any other holiday.

This is the quest that launched this book.

Any quest for Christmas must begin with Christ, of course. But the questions we ask can't be limited to mere religious sentiment or moral allegory. We must delve deeper.

What is the *truth* of Christmas? What really happened 2,000 years ago? Is there any way for readers today to find certainty about what occurred in Bethlehem — or are we left to doubt?

In the quest for Christmas, we will search for truth anywhere it can be found. Given the prominence of the Christmas story throughout the world, many have sought for truth or challenged its claims. These challenges afford us the rare chance to test the claims of Christmas – whether they burn up or endure.

After all, if there is truth to be found in the Christmas story, it should not fear investigation. Real truth fears no challenger, just as real gold fears no fire. Intense heat exposes false gold, but it verifies pure gold, as pure gold has nothing to hide. Real gold emerges from the heat as pure and bright as it entered.

We'll orient our quest for Christmas around a series of challenges testing Christmas from every angle. We'll pass the claims of Christmas through the fire of each challenge, watching to see burn up as lies or emerge pure and bright.

We'll examine the story of Christmas in depth. The Gospels of Matthew and Luke record extensive details about the Christmas events, but few overlap, leading to continuing challenges about their accuracy or authenticity.

We'll take the story to its cultural heart, the longing of every Jewish heart for the coming of Messiah, exploring the challenge of whether or not Jesus fits Jewish expectations – and what that means.

We'll examine the history of Christmas, looking for the evidence of these events in the pages of history. If the

Christmas events happened as the Bible records, then history should not be silent. We'll investigate a series of challenges to the historicity of Christmas, from the census of Quirinius to the Star of Bethlehem to the massacre of the innocents committed by Herod. We'll examine the evidence like detectives studying clues, piecing together the picture of what happened long ago.

We'll examine the prophecy leading up to Christmas. The Old Testament is replete with prophetic declarations about the events of Christmas, identifying who Messiah will be, what He will do, how He will come, and how the world will respond. These prophecies allow us to test the claims of God: either He predicted the future with precision or not.

We'll examine the meaning of Christmas, considering the message conveyed by the stories that have become so familiar to us. Matthew and Luke recorded these stories for specific reasons, intending to reveal specific truths, meanings, and messages. We'll conclude our quest by digging deep into them, searching earnestly for the real meaning of Christmas.

After all, if there is meaning wrapped up in Christmas, it can only be found in truth.

We all want to believe something. We crave hope, we desire meaning, we need love, we strive after peace. But we won't find any of these in Christmas unless we can trust the story we've been given.

This is our quest. The challenges are set before us, testing Christmas at every level. Let's begin.

Christmas awaits.

Challenge One:
The Christmas Story Should Give Up Its Claim to be Historically Accurate

As soon as we embark on our quest for Christmas, resistance rises to meet us.

Yet this resistance is not evil. It means no harm.

Rather it is curious. It seeks truth. It seeks to believe only what is real.

Because of this, what began as resistance can become a source of strength.

Recently a friend of mine launched a long conversation targeting Christmas. To him, the story made little sense. He could accept that some people wanted to believe it, but he could not see how any rational, intelligent person could ever conclude that the story as related in Matthew and Luke happened.

At the heart of our conversation, he said this:

> I would be content to stop at this point if you'd
> agree with the following statement:
>
> "I recognize that my historical and textual
> interpretations are not necessarily the ones that an
> objective, non-sectarian scholar would adopt, but I
> believe they've been revealed to me and other
> believers by God as the true meaning of his
> scriptures."[1]

Can you hear his struggle?

As he saw it, no historian or philosopher would look at the
Christmas story and conclude it happened. He could let
others believe in Christmas if they wanted, as long as we
stopped insisting that the events truly happened.

To be fair to my friend, this kind of doubt is often honest.
It stems from a smart mind that asks fair questions. It's
exactly the kind of mind we want joining us on our quest
for Christmas.

My friend made several good points. If you can't prove that
something happened, how can you convince others it
happened? If you can't verify something you believe, why
should anyone believe it?

This is exactly the kind of doubt that Luke wrote his
Gospel to address. Luke begins his account of the life of

Jesus with the Christmas story, relating in detail how Christ entered the world.

But before Luke begins the story, he takes time to address the need for certainty about truth:

> Inasmuch as many have undertaken to compile a narrative of the things that have been accomplished among us, just as those who from the beginning were eyewitnesses and ministers of the word have delivered them to us, it seemed good to me also, having followed all things closely for some time past, to write an orderly account for you, most excellent Theophilus, that you may have certainty concerning the things you have been taught. (Luke 1:1-4, ESV, emphasis added).

Luke's desire — the passion which drove him to complete his epic account of Jesus' life — was the desire to give his friend certainty about his beliefs.

In the quest for Christmas, certainty matters. If we cannot trust the story we're told, how could it ever change our lives?

Luke never shuns the curious or shames the doubting. Rather, Luke addresses the need for certainty head-on. Luke knows the material he presents will be unique — and to some, difficult to believe.

Luke acknowledges the difficulty inherent in believing the Christmas story, along with the rest of his Gospel. That's why he took such care to consult the eyewitnesses, gather the evidence, and write an orderly account.

Doubt is understandable. We are claiming incredible things to declare that God took on flesh and lived among us.

But what if these events truly happened?

If God truly existed and took on flesh, what would it look like? What would we expect to find in history? How would people respond to such an event — both the powerful and the downtrodden? How would we expect it to change the world?

After all, if Christmas is real, we should be able to verify it.

Matthew and Luke record a Christmas story that happened in real places, at a specific time, involving historical people, with details so unique and far-reaching that they cannot hide in the record of history. If they happened, we should be able to verify them. If they didn't, then we should be able to disprove them. Like detectives, we can examine the evidence and follow it to the truth it reveals, whatever that may be.

This is the way Christianity has presented itself from the beginning. The claims may be incredible, but the evidence is compelling. Therefore, don't take our word for it. Study it for yourself and discover the God waiting at the answer to all your questions.

Paul, whom Luke traveled with extensively, wrote the following to address the same need for certainty Luke addressed:

> I delivered to you as of first importance what I also received: that Christ died for our sins in accordance with the Scriptures, that he was buried, that he was raised on the third day in accordance with the Scriptures, and that he appeared to Cephas, then to the twelve. Then he appeared to more than five hundred brothers at one time, most of whom are still alive, though some have fallen asleep. Then he appeared to James, then to all the apostles. Last of all, as to one untimely born, he appeared also to me. [...]
>
> Now if Christ is proclaimed as raised from the dead, how can some of you say that there is no resurrection of the dead? But if there is no resurrection of the dead, then not even Christ has been raised. And if Christ has not been raised, then our preaching is in vain and your faith is in vain.
>
> [...] if Christ has not been raised, your faith is futile and you are still in your sins. Then those also who have fallen asleep in Christ have perished. If in Christ we have hope in this life only, we are of all

> people most to be pitied. (1 Corinthians 15:3-9, 12-14, 17-19, ESV)

Paul lays the matter out as starkly as possible. If the story of Jesus is fake, then Christianity is worthless — "vain." If Jesus was not the true God who took on flesh, died on the Cross, and rose three days later, then the Christians who believe such things are "of all people most to be pitied."

But if Jesus is who He claimed to be, then these are the matters of "first importance." If God took on flesh to live among us, if this same God died on the Cross for us, and if this same God returned to life to defeat death and open the way to Heaven, then there is no better news.

What could possibly be better?

Death is defeated! Life will continue long after our frail bodies pass away.

Love is eternal! We will live in a true Paradise, loving and being loved by God and all those with us forever.

Hope wins! Everything you've longed for will indeed come true — ultimate meaning, purpose to living, hope beyond death, significance in suffering, love that sees your very soul and cherishes you completely, beauty enduring and wisdom increasing and joy overflowing.

What could possibly be better than this?

Yet Paul and Luke never leave the matter to blind faith. Both encourage their audience: *examine the evidence.*

The quest for Christmas never limits itself to blind belief. Our quest tackles the hardest questions, digging into the best evidence we can find, so that — as Luke promises — we may find certainty.

As Paul declared, if the Jesus story is fake, then it should be discarded. No one should believe a lie.

But if the Jesus story is true — if God became a baby and entered world 2,000 years ago — then we have every possible reason to hope.

Welcome to the quest for Christmas, my friends.

Challenge Two:
Matthew and Luke's Accounts of Jesus' Birth Contradict

Out of the four Gospels, only Matthew and Luke relate the details of Jesus' birth. Yet one challenge emerges immediately upon comparing them: despite relating the same event, they tell almost entirely different stories.

Many challengers to Christmas seize this discrepancy, including Bart Ehrman, one of the most prominent critics of the historicity of the Bible's claims. As he states:

> The stories of Jesus' birth in Matthew 1-2 and Luke 1-2 are very different from each other, and appear to contain down right discrepancies. I don't actually teach this to my students. I instead give them an exercise. If you haven't ever done this, you should try it. I have them list everything that happens, event by event, first in Matthew 1-2 and then in Luke 1-2; and then I have them compare

> their lists. What is similar? What is different? And are any of the differences actual discrepancies that cannot be reconciled?
>
> The differences are striking, and in fact – as I've pointed out on the blog before – some things cannot be reconciled (if Luke is right that the family returned to Nazareth 32 days after the birth [i.e., when the sacrifice that a birthing mother had to give was made], how can Matthew be right that the family fled to Egypt?).[2]

Ehrman lays a challenge, convinced that no student will be able to harmonize the events in both accounts. If so, then he has a point.

After all, if the Bible is true, you should be able to trust *everything* it says. You shouldn't have to pick and choose which version of the Christmas story is true.

Yet Christmas is not so easily laid to rest.

To defeat Ehrman's challenge, all you must do is lay every detail out in chronological order — a tactic Ehrman tries to prevent. Ehrman instructs his students to make two lists of events and compare them side-by-side, as though they reflect similar events at similar times.

But Matthew and Luke record *different* events that happened at *different* times. The solution therefore is to lay them out chronologically in order of when they occurred, not as competing lists.

When you do, Matthew and Luke fit hand-in-glove, each detail supporting each other, uniting to form a grand, seamless story.

Take a few minutes to read the Christmas story anew, this time as one united narrative, in the pages that follow. It's one thing to claim that it all flows together; it's another thing entirely to read it with your own eyes.

After we'll look at a few of the objections people raise and how swiftly this united harmony dispels them.

Matthew 1:18–25a, ESV

> Now the birth of Jesus Christ took place in this way. When his mother Mary had been betrothed to Joseph, before they came together she was found to be with child from the Holy Spirit. And her husband Joseph, being a just man and unwilling to put her to shame, resolved to divorce her quietly. But as he considered these things, behold, an angel of the Lord appeared to him in a dream, saying, "Joseph, son of David, do not fear to take Mary as your wife, for that which is conceived in her is from the Holy Spirit. She will bear a son, and you shall call his name Jesus, for he will save his people from

their sins." All this took place to fulfill what the Lord had spoken by the prophet:

"Behold, the virgin shall conceive and bear a son,
and they shall call his name Immanuel"

(which means, God with us). When Joseph woke from sleep, he did as the angel of the Lord commanded him: he took his wife, but knew her not until she had given birth to a son.

Luke 2:1-20, ESV

In those days a decree went out from Caesar Augustus that all the world should be registered. This was the first registration when Quirinius was governor of Syria. And all went to be registered, each to his own town. And Joseph also went up from Galilee, from the town of Nazareth, to Judea, to the city of David, which is called Bethlehem, because he was of the house and lineage of David, to be registered with Mary, his betrothed, who was with child. And while they were there, the time came for her to give birth. And she gave birth to her firstborn son and wrapped him in swaddling cloths and laid him in a manger, because there was no place for them in the inn.

And in the same region there were shepherds out in the field, keeping watch over their flock by night. And an angel of the Lord appeared to them, and the glory of the Lord shone around them, and they were filled with great fear. And the angel said to them, "Fear not, for behold, I bring you good news of great joy that will be for all the people. For unto you is born this day in the city of David a Savior, who is Christ the Lord. And this will be a sign for you: you will find a baby wrapped in swaddling cloths and lying in a manger." And suddenly there was with the angel a multitude of the heavenly host praising God and saying,

"Glory to God in the highest,
and on earth peace among those with whom he is pleased!"

When the angels went away from them into heaven, the shepherds said to one another, "Let us go over to Bethlehem and see this thing that has happened, which the Lord has made known to us." And they went with haste and found Mary and Joseph, and the baby lying in a manger. And when they saw it, they made known the saying that had been told them concerning this child. And all who heard it wondered at what the shepherds told them. But Mary treasured up all these things, pondering them in her heart. And the shepherds returned, glorifying and praising God for all they had heard and seen, as it had been told them.

Matthew 1:25, Luke 2:21, ESV

And at the end of eight days, when he was circumcised, Joseph called his name Jesus, the name given by the angel before he was conceived in the womb.

Luke 2:22-39, ESV

And when the time came for their purification according to the Law of Moses, they brought him up to Jerusalem to present him to the Lord (as it is written in the Law of the Lord, "Every male who first opens the womb shall be called holy to the Lord") and to offer a sacrifice according to what is said in the Law of the Lord, "a pair of turtledoves, or two young pigeons." Now there was a man in Jerusalem, whose name was Simeon, and this man was righteous and devout, waiting for the consolation of Israel, and the Holy Spirit was upon him. And it had been revealed to him by the Holy Spirit that he would not see death before he had seen the Lord's Christ. And he came in the Spirit into the temple, and when the parents brought in

13

the child Jesus, to do for him according to the custom of the Law, he took him up in his arms and blessed God and said,

"Lord, now you are letting your servant depart in peace, according to your word; for my eyes have seen your salvation that you have prepared in the presence of all peoples, a light for revelation to the Gentiles, and for glory to your people Israel."

And his father and his mother marveled at what was said about him. And Simeon blessed them and said to Mary his mother, "Behold, this child is appointed for the fall and rising of many in Israel, and for a sign that is opposed (and a sword will pierce through your own soul also), so that thoughts from many hearts may be revealed."

And there was a prophetess, Anna, the daughter of Phanuel, of the tribe of Asher. She was advanced in years, having lived with her husband seven years from when she was a virgin, and then as a widow until she was eighty-four. She did not depart from the temple, worshiping with fasting and prayer night and day. And coming up at that very hour she began to give thanks to God and to speak of him to all who were waiting for the redemption of Jerusalem.

And when they had performed everything according to the Law of the Lord, they returned into Galilee, to their own town of Nazareth.

[One to two years pass]
Matthew 2:1-23, ESV

Now after Jesus was born in Bethlehem of Judea in the days of Herod the king, behold, wise men from the east came to Jerusalem, saying, "Where is he who has been born king of the Jews? For we saw his star when it rose and have come to worship him." When Herod the king heard this, he was troubled, and all Jerusalem with him; and assembling all the chief priests and scribes of the people, he inquired of them where the Christ was to be born. They told him, "In Bethlehem of Judea, for so it is written by the prophet:

"'And you, O Bethlehem, in the land of Judah,
are by no means least among the rulers of Judah;
for from you shall come a ruler
who will shepherd my people Israel.'"

Then Herod summoned the wise men secretly and ascertained from them what time the star had appeared. And he sent them to Bethlehem, saying, "Go and search diligently for the child, and when

15

you have found him, bring me word, that I too may come and worship him." After listening to the king, they went on their way. And behold, the star that they had seen when it rose went before them until it came to rest over the place where the child was. When they saw the star, they rejoiced exceedingly with great joy. And going into the house, they saw the child with Mary his mother, and they fell down and worshiped him. Then, opening their treasures, they offered him gifts, gold and frankincense and myrrh. And being warned in a dream not to return to Herod, they departed to their own country by another way.

Now when they had departed, behold, an angel of the Lord appeared to Joseph in a dream and said, "Rise, take the child and his mother, and flee to Egypt, and remain there until I tell you, for Herod is about to search for the child, to destroy him." And he rose and took the child and his mother by night and departed to Egypt and remained there until the death of Herod. This was to fulfill what the Lord had spoken by the prophet, "Out of Egypt I called my son."

Then Herod, when he saw that he had been tricked by the wise men, became furious, and he sent and killed all the male children in Bethlehem and in all that region who were two years old or under, according to the time that he had ascertained from the wise men. Then was fulfilled what was spoken by the prophet Jeremiah:

"A voice was heard in Ramah,
weeping and loud lamentation,
Rachel weeping for her children;
she refused to be comforted, because they are no more."

But when Herod died, behold, an angel of the Lord appeared in a dream to Joseph in Egypt, saying, "Rise, take the child and his mother and go to the land of Israel, for those who sought the child's life are dead." And he rose and took the child and his mother and went to the land of Israel. But when he heard that Archelaus was reigning over Judea in place of his father Herod, he was afraid to go there, and being warned in a dream he withdrew to the district of Galilee. And he went and lived in a city called Nazareth, so that what was spoken by the prophets might be fulfilled, that he would be called a Nazarene.

When every detail is placed in order, Matthew and Luke harmonize beautifully — just as you'd expect if they both strived to record the truth. Their source material differed; Matthew records the experiences of Joseph and the wise men, while Luke records the experiences of Mary and those at the Temple. Yet they all flow together marvelously, complementing each other and informing each other, creating a narrative that almost seems to be the work of a single author.

———

Yet even this inter-woven harmony is not without its challengers.

If there is one central difficulty in this harmony, it is placing the wise men's arrival a year or two after Jesus is born. Most nativities feature the wise men prominently, displaying them arriving the same night as the shepherds.

But if the wise men do arrive so early, then Matthew and Luke cannot both be true. As Ehrman claims:

> [S]ome things cannot be reconciled (if Luke is right that the family returned to Nazareth 32 days after the birth [i.e., when the sacrifice that a birthing mother had to give was made], how can Matthew be right that the family fled to Egypt?)[3]

It's a challenge we must take seriously. To do so, we must take the text seriously. We must study what Matthew and Luke claim, separating their words from the assumptions we often place over them.

When we do, a solution swiftly emerges.

We assume that the wise men arrive on the night Jesus was born, or soon after. Yet Matthew provides three clues to the reader, clueing us in to the length of time that has transpired between Jesus' birth and the wise men's visit.

We find our first clue in Matthew's Gospel clearly stating that the wise men arrived *"after* Jesus was born"* (Matthew 2:1, ESV). Matthew 1:18-25 completes its narration of Jesus' birth, closing with Joseph naming the baby Jesus. Then the action pauses. Matthew 2:1 picks up the story sometime after Jesus' birth. To find out how long after, we need our next two clues.

Our second clue focuses on how Matthew describes Jesus. In Luke 2:12, on the night Jesus was born, the angels describe Jesus as a *brephos* (βρε'φος) — a newborn baby. Yet when the wise men find Jesus, Matthew 2:11 describes him as a *paidion* (παιδι'ον) — a toddler or child. When the wise men worship Jesus, He can stand on His own toddler feet.

Our third clue reveals itself through the midst of tragedy.

Once Herod realizes the wise men hid the location of Jesus from him, he orders the death of every child two years old and under, "according to the time that he had ascertained from the wise men" (Matthew 2:16, ESV). It seems that the wise men expected to find a child around the age of two, or perhaps a child who was conceived two years ago, but was now just over the age of one. (In Chapter 5, on the

Star of Bethlehem, we'll explore the precise data that led them to this conclusion).

This age matches perfectly with the description of Jesus as a *paidion* — a toddler or young child.

Given these three clues, it seems that somewhere between a year or two elapsed since Jesus was born.

But this answer raises its own question: why does Luke state that Mary, Joseph, and Jesus returned to Nazareth a few weeks after His birth, yet Matthew records them living in Bethlehem a year later?

The answer is found in shame.

No one believed Mary's claim that she was pregnant by the Holy Spirit. Even Joseph did not believe until he received his own visit from Gabriel, confirming her story. Everyone in Nazareth assumed that Mary committed adultery.

This heaped a severe measure of shame on Mary's head in the eyes of her neighbors. Women who slept around were often stoned to death to avenge the shame they had brought to their family. Everyone expected the family honor to be maintained at all costs.

This expectation therefore brought even further shame on Joseph, as he refused to submit Mary for stoning. Even before the angelic visit, he wanted to divorce Mary quietly, to spare her life. After the angel visits and the child's birth,

Joseph stood even more committed to protecting his wife and son. To us who know the reasons why, Joseph's actions shine with nobility and self-sacrifice. To the neighbors who did not, Joseph seemed to be a weak-willed coward who wouldn't divorce a wife who cheated on him and who despised his own family's honor.

That placed Mary, Joseph, and Jesus in the most shameful position possible in Nazareth. No family would be more despised — or more in danger.

Given these cultural realities, the flow of events seems clear.

Joseph, Mary, and Jesus returned to Nazareth a few weeks after Jesus' birth, once their dedication at the Temple concluded. They found life in Nazareth to be intolerable, due to the scorn their neighbors heaped on them.

Life in Bethlehem must have seemed marvelous by comparison. After all, they had been celebrated by the local shepherds, which meant they'd be welcomed and protected by all their families. Who wouldn't want to live where they were celebrated, rather than shamed?

It makes perfect sense that after enduring Nazareth's scorn for a few months, Joseph, Mary, and Jesus moved permanently to Bethlehem. They made a life there, protected by those who revered their child, until the wise men arrived a year or so later.

And that simply, we find the Christmas story reconciled.

The evidence paints a clear picture: Matthew and Luke took their work seriously. They each recorded the testimony of their sources faithfully, with such immaculate precision that their work can be inter-woven into one seamless narrative, without a single word added or removed to make it fit.

One may even discern the presence of a divine hand at work — a sole Author telling His story carefully, preserving it faithfully, so that we may find certainty: this Story is unlike any other.

Challenge Three:
Jesus Was Not A Jewish Messiah

One glance through Matthew's Christmas story reveals a host of Old Testament quotations and references. Matthew writes from a Jewish mindset to a Jewish audience, arguing from the Scriptures that Jesus is the Messiah.

Yet many voices throughout the centuries have challenged the Gospel stories, claiming that they reflect Gentile ideas, not Jewish ones. As such, Christmas does not reflect the coming of the Messiah promised in Scripture, but rather a fake Messiah created from pagan ideas interposed over Scripture. As one notable writer stated recently:

> In a world where ideas, beliefs and religious expression have real meaning, it's simply disingenuous to ignore those intrinsic definitions and replace them with whatever just feels cozy. Christmas is not a universal wintertime celebration of gift-giving, lights and tree-decorating. It's a *Christian* holiday celebrating the birth of Jesus, the

> *Christian* Messiah.
>
> But by all Jewish standards, Jesus was not the Messiah.[4]

Many reasons can be given for such a sentiment (and indeed, future chapters in this book will explore the Jewish prophecies and expectations, discussing more of these objections in detail).

But the king of all objections to Jesus being the Jewish Messiah is simply this: Christians claim that Jesus is God.

I was privileged to engage in a fascinating conversation on this matter recently with a skillful Jewish writer. She stated directly:

> "Jesus claims to be the Messiah, the Son of God." If so, he is announcing that he can never be any kind of messiah in any Jewish sense. A messiah can never be a begotten son of God. Neither can anyone else in any Jewish environment or context. In fact, a god that begets offspring, in place of a human father doing the begetting, can never be any part of a Jewish concept or tradition. That begetting is evidence of a non-Jewish story.[5]

There is Scriptural precent for such a belief. The Torah seems to support the idea that God cannot be a human, as it states:

24

> God is not man, that he should lie, or a son of man, that he should change his mind. (Numbers 23:19, ESV)

Isaiah builds on this idea by declaring how transcendent God is. Isaiah records the praises sung of God in Heaven, where the angels declare:

> "Holy, holy, holy is the LORD of hosts; the whole earth is full of his glory!" (Isaiah 6:3, ESV)

If God is Holy, then God is not like humanity. To be holy is to be unique, set apart, distinct. It is to be anything but common, anything but ordinary, anything but normal. To be holy is to be like God, not like man.

Finally, and perhaps most potently to the Jewish faith, the *shema* states with no wiggle room:

> "Hear, oh Israel, the LORD our God, the LORD is one!" (Deuteronomy 6:4, ESV)

If God is one, and God dwells in Heaven, how can a human being standing on Earth claim to be this God? He is a second person, standing on earth, claiming to be the same person who exists in Heaven. This seems impossible to reconcile with such a clear statement that God is only one.

Given verses like these, Jewish skepticism over Jesus' claim to be God is certainly understandable. No one who seeks God wants to believe lies about Him. Worse, no one wants to spread lies about God. To do so is blasphemy, and no one wants to blaspheme the God they worship and adore.

Yet amid all this, Matthew, a Jewish writer, presents an unequivocal claim: Jesus is not only the Jewish Messiah, but is indeed the God whom the Jews worship, who has come in the flesh. Matthew proclaims:

> "She will bear a son, and you shall call his name *Jesus*, for *he will save his people from their sins*." All this took place to fulfill what the Lord had spoken by the prophet: "Behold, the virgin shall conceive and bear a son and they shall call his name Immanuel" (which means, *God with us*). (Matthew 1:21–23, ESV, emphasis added)

Matthew includes two direct claims to this baby Jesus being God.

First, Jesus bears the title Immanuel, meaning "God with us." In the person of this baby, God is with us. This seems straightforward enough, but of course there is wiggle room. Perhaps the name does not mean that God is with us in the direct person of this baby, rather that this baby is a reminder that God is with His people.

Yet Matthew's second claim seems precisely targeted to remove this wiggle room. Gabriel tells Joseph to name the baby "Jesus." In Hebrew, this name means "God saves." Gabriel then gives the reason why the baby must bear this particular name: "He will save his people from their sins."

Did you catch that?

Name *this baby* "God saves" because *this baby* saves.

Many people bore the name Jesus at this time. People loved the reminder that God indeed saves.

But Gabriel did not give this name as a mere reminder that God saves. Gabriel gave this name specifically because *this baby* will save, doing the work the God alone can do.

What, then, are we to think? Is Jesus the Jesus Messiah, or does Matthew's claim that Jesus is God make such a thing impossible?

To find out, let's dig into the Old Testament, examining what exactly the Jewish Scriptures tell us to look for in Messiah.

And let's be clear on the outset: No Christian should ever denigrate the Jewish faith. The Jewish desire to be faithful to the Scriptures is to be celebrated, especially as they cling to the revelation from God in the Torah, wisdom books, and prophets. Jews love the God of Israel, as do Christians, and so we ought to love each other.

After all, Christians are wild branches that have been grafted onto the cultivated vine of God's people (Romans

11:17-24). The Jews are the original vine. The wild branch should never scorn the vine it's grafted onto.

My desire therefore is to honor the Jewish Scriptures and the faith they fuel. I hope to do so by revealing good news of great joy: that the Messiah they long for truly was born in Bethlehem.

———

To begin with, let's explore a familiar Christmas passage from the prophet Isaiah. I'll quote a Jewish translator to help bring out the original sense of the text:

> For **a child is born** to us,
> **a son is given** to us;
> dominion will rest on his shoulders,
> and he will be given the name
> Pele-Yo'etz El Gibbor
> Avi-'Ad Sar-Shalom
> [Wonder of a Counselor, **Mighty God,**
> **Father of Eternity**, Prince of Peace],
> in order to extend the dominion
> and perpetuate the peace
> of the throne and kingdom of David,
> to secure it and sustain it
> through justice and righteousness
> **henceforth and forever.**
> The zeal of Adonai-Tzva'ot [The LORD of Hosts]

> will accomplish this. (Isaiah 9:6-7, Complete
> Jewish Bible, emphasis added)

This passage prophesies the rule and reign of Messiah, the One who will rule the kingdom of David. Yet this is no ordinary ruler. He bears two properties never before united in a single individual.

This Messiah is human: "for a child is born to us."

Yet this Messiah is also God: He is "Mighty God," the "Father of Eternity."

To fulfill this prophecy, Messiah must be more than human. He will reign on David's throne in peace and righteousness "forever." He does not merely establish the kingdom, then leave it to His descendants. Rather, this Messiah Himself secures and sustains the throne and kingdom of David henceforth and forever — from now throughout eternity.

This Messiah must be a human child to be a proper descendent of David.

Yet He must also be more than human. He must be able to rule and reign forever, in full righteousness and peace — something only God can do.

Yet here the pushback is clear: how can God become a man? How can a God so holy and so transcendent become like us?

In the beginning, God told of another way. He spoke not of God becoming like humans, but rather of humans being made like God, in His own image:

> Then God said, "Let us make humanity in our image, after our likeness." (Genesis 1:26)

When God created humanity, designing us from the atom on up, He fashioned us after His own image. This requires that God had an image before He made us, such that He could make us like it.

God made us in His own image, bodies and all. In the person of Jesus, God did not change to became like us. Rather, in the person of Jesus, God revealed the image He fashioned humanity after.

Can God appear in human form?

Of course. Human form is fashioned after Him.

Yet some may question; how can we be certain that having a body is part of what it means to be made in God's image?

Certainly, being made in God's image is a rich idea, one we could dig into endlessly. But the Scriptures provide several clues that possessing a body is indeed a central part of it.

Our first clue appears on page one. When God first declares that He will make humanity in His image, He immediately makes an embodied human. God does not fashion humanity as a bodiless soul or an ethereal mind. Humans possessed bodies from the first moment after being made in God's image.

Our second clue emerges as we follow Adam and Eve through their story. Familiar language appears at the beginning of their family line:

> When God created humanity, He made them in the likeness of God. Male and female He created them, and He blessed them and named them Man when they were created. When Adam lived 130 years, he fathered a son in his own likeness, after his image, and named him Seth. (Genesis 5:1-3, ESV)

Genesis 5 deliberately pairs two creations made in the likeness of their creators. God made male and female in His likeness, even as Adam and Eve created Seth in their own likeness, after their image. It would be strange indeed if "likeness" had no connection to a body in the first use, but a verse later was intrinsically connected to bodies.

Our third clue is found in the nature of God: God doesn't change.

If God is eternal, then God does not change. If Jesus is "the same yesterday, today, and forever" (Hebrews 13:8,

NIV), then He did not become something new when He took on flesh. If Jesus truly is God, and Jesus has a body now, then He has had a body for all eternity.

And indeed, we find glimpses of this eternal body throughout the Scriptures. When Isaiah is taken into the presence of God, he witnesses the angels proclaiming the holiness of God. In the midst of them, Isaiah testifies:

> I saw the LORD sitting upon a throne, high and lifted up, and the train of His robe filled the Temple. (Isaiah 6:1, ESV)

To sit on a throne, you must have a body. Likewise, to wear a robe, you must have a body. There is no doubt this is God he sees, and that this God exists with a body.

If God therefore has a body, and He created our bodies after His image, then what is there to prevent Him from appearing in a body among us?

Some may answer using the three verses we began with. They may argue, as the angels in Isaiah 6:3 declare, that God is "Holy, holy, holy!" He cannot take on flesh and dwell among such a sinful people, as though He were common.

Yet holiness is not opposed to humanity, as though they could never coincide. In Genesis 1 and 2, before sin entered the world, God dwelled with humanity in perfect peace. God's holiness never kept Him apart from His children.

Holiness is opposed to sin. To be made holy, we don't have to be cleansed from being human. We must be cleansed from our sin. God washes our sin away, making us holy by the blood of a spotless sacrifice — perfect blood, shed to reunite us to the God who loves us and made us in His image, as every baby is made in the image of its parents.

A second objection may arise, stating in the words of Deuteronomy 6:4 "the LORD is one." God is *one*, not two or three. Jesus therefore cannot be a second God, because there is only one.

Yet the Christmas story does not claim that Jesus is second God. Jesus never claimed to be the offspring of God or a procreated half-God half-human hybrid. Jesus claimed to be God who has come in the flesh, the same God who made us in His image. In His flesh, Jesus revealed the image He fashioned us after.

Finally, others may object using Numbers 23:19: "God is not man, that he should lie, or a son of man, that he should change his mind." How much clearer could it be that God is not man?

Yet that statement is not the end of the verse. It does not simply say "God is not a man," then end the discussion. The point is God's faithfulness, that He keeps His word:

"God is not a man, that He should lie." Humans may lie, and do so every day, yet God never will.

Thus, God will be faithful to His word. Therefore, when God states through the prophet Isaiah that a child will be born who is Mighty God, the Father of Eternity, He means what He says.

This child will be born. He will live as a human.

Yet this child will be so much more than human. He will be the Mighty God, creator of the universe, dwelling within the world His own hands fashioned. He will be the Father of Eternity, the God who commands the end from the beginning, the God who rules forever in eternity yet endlessly loves His children who dwell in time. He loves them so passionately that He would enter time as a baby, live as a human, and die on a Cross, shedding His perfect blood to cleanse His people from their sins.

He did this to open the door to eternity, to bring His children back home.

After all, He made them in His image.

Challenge Four:
Luke Blundered On The History of Quirinius' Census

If you can't trust the Bible on the matters you can verify, how can you trust it on those you can't?

The Bible claims to be a book recording real history. More than that, it claims that the events it records are so significant and so reliable that you can stake your eternal life on them being true.

Luke states as much in the beginning of his Gospel:

> Inasmuch as many have undertaken to compile a narrative of the things that have been accomplished among us, just as those who from the beginning were eyewitnesses and ministers of the word have delivered them to us, it seemed good to me also, having followed all things closely for some time past, to write an orderly account for you, most

excellent Theophilus, that you may have certainty concerning the things you have been taught. (Luke 1:1-4, ESV)

In his own words, Luke sets out to write an orderly account, relying on eyewitnesses, to give certainty about all that has been taught about Jesus.

Yet critical scholars rake Luke across the coals for his depiction of the Christmas story. Even distinguished Christian scholars, such as Raymond Edward Brown, state:

> There are formidable historical difficulties about every facet of Luke's description and dating of the Quirinius census, and most critical scholars acknowledge a confusion and misdating on Luke's part.[6]

He summarizes the problem:

> [...] Difficulties are that there was no single census of the whole Roman Empire under Augustus, and that there is no evidence that Roman censuses required one to go to one's place of ancestry (unless one had property there). More serious is Luke's connection between the reign of Herod the Great (1:5) and the census under Quirinius. Herod died in 4 B.C; Quirinius become governor in Syria and conducted the first Roman census of Judea in A.D.

> 6-7 — and notice it was a census of Judea, not of Galilee as Luke assumes.[7]

If Luke blunders this badly on matters we can check, how can we trust him on any other matter? If Luke fails as a historian, how can a reader ever receive "certainty about the things you have been taught" through his words?

The problem feels hopeless. Yet it hinges on a single word: "If."

If Luke blunders on his history, then we are indeed in trouble. But what if he doesn't?

What if, the further we dig into the raw evidence of history, we find that Luke knew exactly what he was talking about? If history ends up verifying Luke down to the letter, would it give us back our confidence to trust his account of all Jesus said and did?

Let's dive into the history and find out.

———

Let's begin by examining what Luke says, so we know precisely what to corroborate:

> In the days of Herod, king of Judea [...] a decree went out from Caesar Augustus that all the world should be registered. This was the first registration when Quirinius was governor [*hēgemoneuontos*] of

> Syria. And all went to be registered, each to his own town. And Joseph also went up from Galilee, from the town of Nazareth, to Judea, to the city of David, which is called Bethlehem, because he was of the house and lineage of David, to be registered with Mary, his betrothed, who was with child. (Luke 1:5, 2:1–5, ESV)

Thus, we need to see verified:

1. Caesar Augustus decreeing that all the world (under his control) should be registered

2. Quirinius occupying a high office [*hēgemoneuontos*] in Syria during this registration

3. *Two* registrations occurring while Quirinius occupied a high office in Syria, such that one can be said to be "the first"

4. Rome including subject kingdoms like Israel in this registration

5. Rome requiring people to return to their family property to be registered

6. Herod dying *after* these events took place

Easy enough.

———

Point #1: Did Caesar Augustus ever issue a decree around this time?

He did indeed. Ernest Martin summarizes six individual historical witnesses who testify to it:

> There is a reference to such a registration of all the Roman people not long before 5 February 2 B.C. written by Caesar Augustus himself:
>
> "While I was administering my thirteenth consulship [2 B.C.] the senate and the equestrian order and *the entire Roman people* gave me the title Father of my Country" (Res Gestae 35, italics added). This award was given to Augustus on 5 February 2 B.C., therefore the registration of citizen approval must have taken place in 3 B.C.
>
> Orosius, in the fifth century, also said that Roman records of his time revealed that a census was indeed held when Augusts was made "the first of men" —an apt description of his award "Father of the Country" —at a time when all the great nations gave an oath of obedience to Augustus (6:22, 7:2). Orosius dated the census to 3 B.C.
>
> Josephus substantiates that an oath of obedience to Augustus was required in Judea not long before the death of Herod (Antiquities 17:41-45). This agrees nicely in a chronological sense with what

Luke records. But more than that, an inscription found in Paphlagonia (eastern Turkey), also dated to 3 B.C., mentions an "oath sworn by all the people in the land at the altars of Augustus in the temples of Augustus in the various districts."

And dovetailing precisely with this inscription, the early (fifth century) Armenian historian, Moses of Khoren, said the census that brought Joseph and Mary to Bethlehem was conducted by Roman agents in Armenia where they set up "the image of Augustus Caesar in every temple." The similarity of this language is strikingly akin to the wording on the Paphlagonian inscription describing the oath taken in 3 B.C.

These indications can allow us to reasonably conclude that the oath (of Josephus, the Paphlagonian inscription, and Orosius) and the census (mentioned by Luke, Orosius, and Moses of Khoren) were one and the same. All of these things happened in 3 B.C.[8]

Thus we find our first criterion met.

Caesar Augustus did indeed issue an Empire-wide decree in 3 B.C. that all the world should be registered. All the people swore an oath of obedience before a statue of August to confer upon him the title "Father of my Country." Augustus sought to aggrandize himself, yet his

40

self-aggrandizement served the purposes of God, corroborating the account of Jesus' birth.

So far, Luke is spot-on.

Point #2: Did Quirinius hold a high office in Syria at this time, such that he could be referred to as *hēgemoneuontos* of Syria?

He did indeed.

The historians Tacitus and Strabo record that Quirinius led a campaign against the Homonadenses from 12 to 1 B.C. This tribe lived in the Taurus Mountains in Asia Minor, right next door to Syria. To fight this war, Quirinius' legions would have to come from Syria, as it was the only location nearby where legions were permanently stationed. As such, Quirinius' office would be held in Syria, the local bastion of Roman power.

Quirinius led this campaign as a legate sent by the Roman Senate, a diplomatic representative with military authority. This gave Quirinius political power on par with a local governor.[9]

Luke assigns Quirinius the title of *hēgemoneuontos*, often translated "governor." Yet the word refers broadly to the act of governing, rather than to the specific office of "governor."

Thus, history places Quirinius exactly where Luke says he was: occupying one of the most powerful offices in Syria in the final years of Herod's reign.

So far, Luke is 2 for 2.

Point #3: Did *two* registrations occur while Quirinius held office in Syria, such that one could be said to be "the first?"

Indeed they did.

Quirinius' infamous census occurred in 6/7 A.D. It led to many Jewish people revolting under the command of Judas of Galilee, as they held that a census ran contrary to God's commands.

A few years after the census concluded, Quirinius' tenure as legate of Syria ended. No additional census could fit in this narrow gap.

Where, then, is the first census?

Right in 3–2 B.C., as point #1 demonstrates. This was the first registration that occurred while Quirinius occupied one of the highest offices in Syria.

This serves as a major weakness for the argument that Luke could only be referring to the census of 6/7 A.D. If only one census occurred under Quirinius, why would Luke refer to it as "the first?"

But if two registrations occurred while Quirinius held high office in Syria, Luke's words make perfect sense. Given the plentiful evidence for Augustus' Empire-wide oath in 3/2 B.C., we find Luke verified yet again. Two registrations indeed occurred under Quirinius: one in 3/2 BC, and another in 6/7 AD.

Luke is 3 for 3.

Point#4: Did Rome ever take a census in subject kingdoms like Israel?

Despite the objections of many skeptics today, including Raymond Brown, as quoted above, Rome did precisely this.

Tacitus tells us plainly:

> [Augustus] ordered a document to be produced and read. This contained a description of the resources of the State, **of the number of citizens** and allies under arms, of the fleets, **subject kingdoms**, provinces, taxes, direct and indirect, necessary expenses and customary bounties. All these details Augustus had written with his own hand, and had added a counsel, that the empire should be confined to its present limits, either from fear or out of jealousy.[10]

Like most rulers, Augustus desired to know how extensive

his kingdom was. He sought to know the "number of citizens" in his direct rulership, as well as those in "subject kingdoms," such as Israel was in the time of Herod.

Archaeology continues to verify that Rome indeed commanded registrations in subject kingdoms:

> [Critics do not suppose] that Augustus would have a census taken in Palestine during Herod's reign. Certainly Herod had enough autonomy as indicated by his being allowed to mint coins. **However, the Romans did take a census in vassal kingdoms.** In fact, in Venice a gravestone of a Roman officer was found which states that he was ordered by P. Sulpicius Quirinius to conduct a census of Apamea, a city of 117,000 inhabitants, located on the Orontes in Syria, which was an autonomous city-state that minted its own copper coins. In A.D. 36 under Tiberius a census was imposed on the client kingdom of Archelaus of Cappadocia. Again, the powerful Nabatean kings in Petra, who had the right to mint coins were, it seems, obliged to have the Roman financial officers in their domain.[11]

If the clear evidence of history tells us that Rome indeed conducted censuses in their subject kingdoms, we have no reason to doubt it.

Luke continues his track record for accuracy, hitting 4 out of 4 targets thus far.

Point #5: Did Rome require people to return to their hometowns to be registered?

Indeed Rome did.

Critics attack Luke's record constantly over this detail. Why would Rome require people to go to their ancestral hometowns? Why would Rome care whether a person was registered in Nazareth or Bethlehem? Critics claim that no evidence exists for Rome issuing such a command, supposing instead that Luke invented the travel requirement as a narrative device to move Mary and Joseph to Bethlehem.

But archaeology defends Luke beautifully.

Archaeologists continue to uncover plentiful documents relating to censuses and registrations, as governments tend to keep extensive records. These documents shed light on the subject, like Papyrus 904:

> Gaius Vibius Maximus, Praefect of Egypt, states: "The enrollment by household being held, it is necessary to notify all who, for any cause whatsoever, are outside their homes to return to their domestic hearths, that they may also accomplish the customary dispensation of

enrollment and continue steadfastly in husbandry that belongs to them."[12]

Rome commanded people to return to their "domestic hearths" for the purpose of registration.

Why?

A common-sense explanation pops quickly to mind. Israelites kept tight records on ancestral property. According to the Law, all property reverted back to its ancestral owners every 50 years in the year of Jubilee.

If a government wanted to reduce the risk of counting people twice, a natural solution would be to require people to register in the location of their ancestral land.

In our modern world of digital record-keeping, such a requirement seems burdensome. We simply send record-keepers door-to-door to record how many people live in each home.

But a Roman registration placed the burden on the people being registered. As Moses of Khoren and the Paphlagonian inscription (quoted in point #1 above) testify, Rome required its citizens to go to the local temple or government center to swear the oath before a statue of Augustus. Rome allowed a broad window of 1-2 years for citizens to fulfill their obligation. At the conclusion of the window, any citizen who had not registered could be punished.

If Rome allowed people to register wherever they pleased, it would be nearly impossible to track people accurately.

But if Rome required each Israelite to register in the city of their ancestral land, they could track each person with relative ease. Given the logic of such a strategy, and the proof that Rome employed such a strategy in Egypt at this time, we have every reason to expect that Rome employed the same requirement in Israel.

Luke moves to a comfortable 5 for 5.

Point #6: Did Herod die after these events?

Indeed, this seems the most likely conclusion.

Many historians assert that Herod died in 4 B.C., which would make Luke's chronology impossible. Yet the evidence upon which they build this claim proves to be its undoing.

Outside of the Bible, the historian Josephus provides the abundance of our evidence regarding the death of Herod. Josephus provides two clear bookends within which to locate Herod's death: a lunar eclipse preceded Herod's death, while Passover followed it.

A partial eclipse occurred on March 13 of 4 B.C, a mere 29 days before Passover. Those who hold to the 4 B.C. date for Herod's death claim this to be the eclipse Josephus mentioned, yet two problems swiftly arise:

- The eclipse was barely visible in Israel. It was most visible in Africa.

- Josephus records a wealth of activity occurring after the eclipse and before Herod's death, which cannot fit in a mere 29 days.

Is there a better candidate for the eclipse?

Indeed there is.

In January 10 of 1 B.C., Israel observed a dramatic full eclipse. This means:

- Everyone in Israel witnessed it, unlike the eclipse in 4 B.C.

- It occurred early enough in the year for all the events Josephus records to occur before Passover

Other details can be mentioned, but the heart of the matter is established clearly by these bookends, as we can verify them with precision.

The evidence seems to favor Herod dying in 1 B.C., allowing full time for a census to occur in 3/2 B.C., Joseph and Mary to travel to Egypt with Jesus, and dwell there for a time before returning after Herod's death.

This allows Luke to clear the last hurdle, being verified 6 out of 6 times.

———

Luke, therefore, is a fantastic historian. Despite the claims of many, each of his data points regarding the birth of Jesus can be verified in the historical record.

It seems that Luke indeed took care to write an orderly account, that we may have certainty regarding the things he teaches of the life and ministry of Jesus. History backs him up every step of the way.

Challenge Five:
No Star Can Do What the Star of Bethlehem Does

If there was one aspect of the Christmas story that was most likely to be mythological, it would be the Star of Bethlehem.

It appears to do what no star can do: it tells the wise men that the Messiah is born, it leads them to Israel, it hovers over the house where Mary, Joseph, and Jesus are found. How can a star do such things?

Critics are quick to label such ideas as fanciful, invented by the Gospel writers to make Jesus' birth seem more significant. Even Christians who believe the Bible aren't sure how to deal with the Star. Some believe it to be a comet or meteor; others say it was simply a supernatural, one-time event.

But what if the Star of Bethlehem was truly historical? What if we could examine the evidence through the lens of modern astronomy and prove that the Star was real — and that it did everything Matthew's Gospel records?

If such a thing were possible, it would be a tremendous boost to the historicity of the Christmas story. It would prove that you could take even the most seemingly impossible details, examine them intensely, and find that they prove true.

Is such a thing possible?

Let's examine the evidence together to find out.

———

Let me make a seemingly crazy statement, then spend the rest of the chapter defending it:

The Star of Bethlehem is Jupiter.

At first, that sounds ridiculous. Jupiter is a planet, not a star. Further, how could Jupiter lead the way for the wise men, or come to rest over Bethlehem?

To begin, let's examine the Greek word Matthew uses to describe the Star: *astera*. This word can refer to a traditional star, of course, but also to a planet (a moving star), or a comet or meteor. Thus any of these celestial bodies could potentially be the *astera* of which Matthew speaks.

To take this one step further, and prove that the Star was in fact Jupiter, we turn to astronomy. Using modern software, we can recreate the sky from 2,000 years ago. When we do, we can watch Jupiter perform every action that Matthew's Gospel describes it performing.

It's simply stunning.

Matthew describes the Star of Bethlehem with ten key details:

> Now after Jesus was born in Bethlehem of Judea in the days of Herod the king, behold, wise men from the east came to Jerusalem, saying, "Where is he who has been **born king** of the **Jews**? For we saw his **star in the east** and have come to **worship** him." (Matthew 2:1–2, ESV)

From these two verses, we glean five details:

1. The star signified *kingship*

2. The star pointed to a King being from the *Jewish people*

3. The star pointed to the King being *born*

4. The star rose *in the east*, like most stars do

5. The wise men intended to *worship* the person this star signified

A few verses later, we find a few additional clues:

> When Herod the king heard this, he was troubled, and all Jerusalem with him [...] Then Herod summoned the wise men secretly and ascertained from them **what time the star had appeared.** (Matthew 2:3,7, ESV)

Thus we can tell:

6. The star appeared *at an exact time that could be verified*

7. Herod and all those in Jerusalem *missed it completely*

These two details abolish the idea that the star could be a comet or some supernatural glowing light pointing to Bethlehem. If it had been something this obvious, everyone would have known about it, yet Herod was clueless.

Whatever the star was, it was easy to miss if you weren't paying attention.

Many movies depict the star as a giant glowing object (typically shaped like a cross) with a ray of light pointing straight to Jesus' manger. But such a sign would be impossible to miss at night in a society with few night-time lights.

The next few verses give us our final three clues:

> And he sent them to Bethlehem, saying, "Go and search diligently for the child, and when you have found him, bring me word, that I too may come and worship him." After listening to the king, they went on their way. And behold, **the star that they had seen** when it rose went before them until **it came to rest over the place where the child was**. When they saw the star, they rejoiced exceedingly with great joy (Matthew 2:8–10, ESV)

From this, we can conclude:

8. The star *endured over a long period of time*

The wise men had seen it in the East and traveled to Israel, yet the star was still visible to them from Jerusalem.

9. The star *went ahead of them* on the journey from Jerusalem to Bethlehem

10. The star *stopped* in the sky above the place where the child was

Let's take these ten details and compare them to Jupiter as it dances through the ancient Israelite sky.

For our first three points, the star needs to perform an action that signifies *kingship, birth, and the Jewish people*. Does Jupiter do such a thing?

Indeed it does.

Ancient astronomers always associated Jupiter with royalty, given its status as the largest planet that moved through the night sky. Jupiter is the King Planet.

Likewise, Regulus was the King Star. It shone brighter than nearly anything else in the nighttime sky. (Today, we can zoom in and discern that Regulus is a group of *four* stars which exist so closely together that they appeared to be a singular entity to the unaided eye. This four-fold brightness explains why it outshone all else, reigning as the King Star).

Jupiter passes Regulus once every 12 years. Typically, they pass and go on their merry ways.

But in 3 B.C. they performed something spectacular.

Jupiter passes Regulus, as always. Then it loops back around and passes Regulus a second time. Then it loops back around a third time and completes a third pass by Regulus — in effect, drawing a crown:

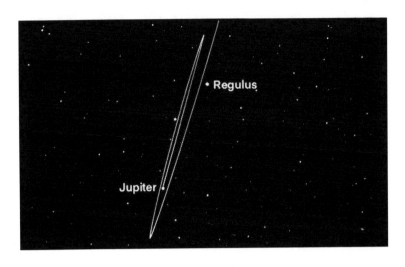

In September of 3 B.C., the King Planet drew a crown around the King Star.

This triple conjunction is so rare that no astronomer watching it would ever have witnessed it before. Yet anyone randomly looking up at the night sky would see nothing different. There was no supernova burst or comet streaking by. But to an astronomer who studied the night sky constantly, the King Planet broke protocol to crown the King Star, a literal once-in-a-lifetime event.

This matches our first data point. The King Planet crowning the King Star certainly signifies *kingship*.

But where is our connection to the *Jewish people?* For that, we look back to Genesis:

> Judah is a lion's cub; from the prey, my son, you
> have gone up. He stooped down; he crouched as a

> lion and as a lioness; who dares rouse him? The scepter shall not depart from Judah, nor the ruler's staff from between his feet, until tribute comes to him; and to him shall be the obedience of the peoples. (Genesis 49:9–10, ESV)

From the beginning, Judah's tribe bore the symbol of the lion. This symbolism carried over as Israel's identity became uniquely Jewish. Even the modern-day emblem of Jerusalem features the Lion of Judah front and center.

Thus, when the coronation occurs within the constellation of Leo, the Lion, it points straight to Judah. The coronation even occurred on the Jewish New Year, further strengthening the connection.

So far, we have a clear *kingship* and we have a clear link to the *Jewish people*. But what about the star signifies *birth*? If this conjunction signified a conception of a new king, we should expect something to happen nine months later.

Indeed, precisely nine months after the coronation, Jupiter the King Planet is birthed out of Venus, the Mother Planet.

In June of 2 B.C., Jupiter approached Venus. Both planets shone at their brightest. When they neared, they did not cover each other, but aligned immediately next to each other, in effect forming a number 8. This allowed them to add their full brilliance to each other, neither eclipsing the other. On June 17 of 2 B.C. the King Planet and the Mother Planet becoming the brightest star in the nighttime sky. This is the day of Jesus' birth.

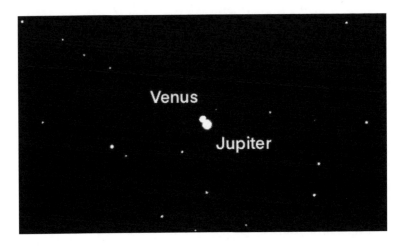

Planetariums around the globe replay this conjunction often around Christmastime. It's a fantastic show.

With these three points, we have *kingship*, the *Jewish people*, and *birth*. The coronation signifies conception, and nine months later the King Planet emerges from the Mother Planet in the brightest display in the nighttime sky.

These actions also meet four further qualifications:

- The star rose *in the east*, just as most stars do.

- The star appeared *at a precise time*, such that anyone making note of the paths of the planets could reproduce it from their observations.

- The star was visible, but it was *missed completely* by Herod and everyone in Jerusalem. To anyone not paying attention, the stars shone as they always do. But to astronomers, the symbology crackled with meaning.

- The star *endured over time*, such that the wise men could witness the coronation and birth in the sky, then travel to Jerusalem to seek out this newborn king, where they saw it again.

That meets seven qualifications.

Yet now we have a seemingly impossible task: the star must *go ahead of the wise men to Bethlehem* and *stop in the sky* above the place where Jesus was born.

Could Jupiter ever do such a thing?

After the wise men witnessed the conjunction of Jupiter and Venus in June of 2 BC, they began traveling. Such a journey would take months, particularly if they left from the regions around Babylon, where many people of Jewish descent lived at the time.

It's reasonable to suppose that they arrived at Jerusalem in December of 2 BC. If they did, and they looked south to Bethlehem (which lay a mere five miles away), they witnessed Jupiter standing directly above Bethlehem in the night sky.

Or to say it directly:

Jupiter led the way straight from Jerusalem to Bethlehem.

But to fulfill what Matthew describes, Jupiter needed to *stop* in the sky. Can a planet do that?

Indeed it can, and it did.

The wise men proceeded first to Jerusalem, the capital city, supposing that the newborn King would be in the palace. Herod and the scribes pointed the wise men to Bethlehem, as Micah's prophecy required the Messiah to be born there.

As the wise men left Jerusalem and looked to Bethlehem, they saw Jupiter hanging immediately above the tiny village.

But Jupiter stood at a unique place in its orbit. Before the eyes of the wise men, Jupiter entered retrograde motion. In other words, it was traveling in one direction across the sky. Then it stopped and went back the way it came.

And you'll never guess when this happened.

On December 25th of 2 BC, Jupiter stopped in the sky directly over Bethlehem.

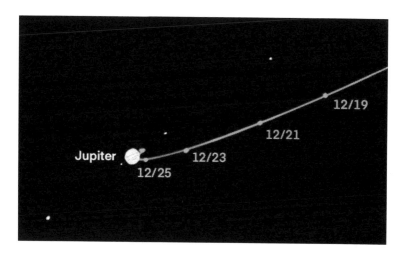

Bethlehem was only five miles from Jerusalem. When the wise men saw that the star had stopped in the sky over Bethlehem, they rode swiftly to the village, found Jesus, and offered Him their gifts. December 25th truly was the first Christmas.

One detail remains: *worship*. The wise men came not merely to pay homage to this newborn King, but to worship Him.

This prompts the question: who were these wise men? Why were they studying the sky, intending to worship the one the stars revealed?

The book of Daniel describes how the Jewish people not only survived their exile in Babylon — but thrived. Daniel rose to the highest echelons of power in the land, all while being a supremely faithful Jew. As a result, he was able to provide a decent living to his fellow Jews. The longer their exile endured, the better life became.

61

When the Exile ended and God returned His people to their homeland, many stayed behind. Life was good, and the city of Babylon (now part of Persia) was prosperous. Daniel's shadow loomed large over the Jews who remained, as his faithfulness to God and service to these foreign powers led to their own prosperity.

The dots seem to connect rather directly. Daniel's spiritual descendants remained in Babylon, being faithful Jews as he strived to be. Daniel led an exceedingly wise life, such that he served as a chief advisor and administrator in two distinct empires. It is likely many of his spiritual descendants followed in his footsteps, leading similarly wise lives.

Some of these wise men studied the night sky. They studied the Hebrew Scriptures, as Daniel had done, paying attention to all they declared about who the Messiah would be.

In the years of 3/2 B.C., the heavens declared the glory of God and the arrival of His Messiah. These wise men knew the Hebrew Scriptures. They knew to associate the Lion with the tribe of Judah. They knew that Daniel prophesied the birth of a King, Messiah the Prince, around this time. They knew that this King, even as a helpless baby, deserved their worship.

700 years before the star began singing in the night sky, Isaiah the prophet revealed who this King would be:

> For to us a child is born, to us a son is given; [...] and his name shall be called Wonderful Counselor, **Mighty God**, Everlasting Father, Prince of Peace. (Isaiah 9:6, ESV)

The wise men worshiped this King, believing that He was Mighty God, the Everlasting Father, come in the flesh.

This baby is Jesus — Christ the Lord.

For generations, skeptics assumed the Star of Bethlehem was a fairytale, invented to add color to the Christmas story. After all, it did seem outlandish. A star stopping in the sky? A king's birth foretold in the stars? Maybe it fits in the pages of Harry Potter, but not in the pages of history.

Until astronomy proved it to be true.

The Bible is far more accurate than we give it credit for. Every single detail about the Star of Bethlehem proves true.

If we can verify such seemingly obscure details, finding them perfectly accurate beyond expectation, what can we dare to hope about the rest?

Challenge Six:
The Overly-Dramatized Christmas Story is Difficult to Believe

In the quest for Christmas, nostalgia may prove to be one of the worst obstacles to belief.

We love our Christmas stories. Churches hold nativity plays every year, as they have for generations, telling the same beloved story. The audience could likely recite the lines by heart along with the actors on stage. We all sing our Christmas songs and watch our Christmas movies eagerly, celebrating the story we know so well.

But in the generations of re-telling this story, subtle errors have crept into our imaginations. The desire to dramatize the events overtakes even the most pious of storytellers. Over the years, these accumulations slowly begin to distort the Christmas story, until what we see on the stage and what we read on the page bear little resemblance.

This is a tricky matter to untangle. Again, we love these stories. We cherish our manger scenes, our Christmas decorations, and our holiday traditions. Attempting to bring any sort of correction to them is to tread on sacred ground.

Yet we must approach these stories with a renewed desire to understand them accurately. The watching world listens to the stories we tell. If they find the stories hard to believe… they won't.

In a conversation recently over the reliability of the Bible, one friend of mine put it this way:

> So let me get this straight: Joseph voluntarily forced his 9-month pregnant wife to walk 90 miles so that his son could be born in a stable with barn animals, when he was under no compulsion to do so and could have gone any time at his convenience?[13]

Can you hear his struggle?

In our desire to dramatize the Christmas story — to tell it with as much emotion, excitement, and tension as possible — we have altered the story to the point that those outside the church find it difficult to believe.

In the quest for Christmas, historical truth matters to the curious. We must understand the story as the Gospel writers expected their audience to understand it. This may take a bit of work. After all, the Gospel writers wrote nearly two thousand years ago, into a culture with wildly different expectations and assumptions than our own.

In this chapter, we'll attempt to clear away a bit of the rubble that's accumulated over the years. We'll attempt to recover the Christmas story as Matthew and Luke meant it to be understood. The story they tell is dynamic, and well worthy of our time.

Does this mean that we must do away with any of our Christmas pageants that don't get the story exactly right? Of course not. Any telling that celebrates the birth of Jesus and proclaims glory to God is worthy of being told.

But let's take a moment to satisfy the curiosity of those outside the church. Let's examine the history around the Christmas story and let the original message come into a clearer focus.

This story is so familiar to us.

Let's take a chance to explore it anew.

———

We'll begin by focusing on Luke 2. As a test to detect how much we've dramatized the story, take a moment to read the story, below. After, we'll examine what appeared in your imagination and compare it to what the text records.

Luke writes:

66

All went to be registered, each to his own town. And Joseph also went up from Galilee, from the town of Nazareth, to Judea, to the city of David, which is called Bethlehem, because he was of the house and lineage of David, to be registered with Mary, his betrothed, who was with child. And while they were there, the time came for her to give birth. And she gave birth to her firstborn son and wrapped him in swaddling cloths and laid him in a manger, because there was no place for them in the inn. (Luke 2:3–7, ESV)

As you read those words, what did you see in your imagination? Most of us picture something like the following:

- Mary begins to feel labor pains the same day they arrive in town

- A mean innkeeper refuses to let the family in (and nobody in the inn chooses to give up their space)

- Mary and Joseph find a dirty stable out back they can use

- Mary gives birth in the stable with only Joseph there to help

- They lay Jesus in a wooden manger while the animals look on

These details are so familiar that we'd never question them. Yet none of them appear in Luke's account. We've made them all up.

If you felt a sudden urge to check the verses again, you're not alone. I did, too, when this was first pointed out to me. But it's true. Luke does not mention a stable, an innkeeper, or Mary giving birth as soon as they arrive. Luke relates a far more sensible narrative — one that lacks much of the dramatic tension of our imagination, but one that makes far more sense in the real world.

Let's ask a few questions to unravel Luke's true account from our wild imaginations.

When did Mary and Joseph arrive in Bethlehem?

Many Christmas movies depict Mary and Joseph arriving in Bethlehem on the same night she gives birth. From a dramatic standpoint, it makes sense. In a play, it's easier to portray events as though they happen on the same day, rather than stretching them out over months. It also heightens the tension to depict Joseph rushing to find accommodations while Mary is in labor.

But while this dramatizes the action, it portrays Joseph as either inconsiderate or incapable. Either he isn't capable of traveling at a sensible time and finding lodging for his family, or he isn't considerate enough to travel when it's best for Mary.

Luke describes a far more considerate and capable Joseph. He travels with Mary to Bethlehem not in her ninth month of pregnancy, but much earlier. Luke states:

> And Joseph also went up from Galilee, from the town of Nazareth, to [...] Bethlehem, because he was of the house and lineage of David, to be registered with Mary, his betrothed, who was with child. And *while they were there*, the time came for her to give birth. (Luke 2:4-6 ESV)

Joseph and Mary settle into Bethlehem and spend a considerable amount of time there prior to giving birth — a few weeks at the least, but more likely several months, as travel would be easier for Mary the earlier in her pregnancy they could go.

The timeline affords Joseph and Mary plenty of space. After Gabriel informs Mary that she will become pregnant by the Holy Spirit, she travels to her cousin Elizabeth's home. Mary stays there about three months, then returns to Nazareth (Luke 1:39, 56).

When she returns, she is discovered to be with child (Matthew 1:18). This likely happened immediately, in her third or fourth month, as there was little room to hide in the small first-century Jewish homes. How well could a woman hide her pregnancy from her mother, father, and siblings, when they all lived, ate, and slept in a small, one-room house?

Once they discovered Mary's pregnancy (and in a small town, gossip travels swiftly), Joseph is forced to decide how he will respond. At this time, Gabriel visits him, and Joseph realizes this child is the Christ (Matthew 1:19-23).

Immediately upon receiving the news, Joseph brought Mary home as his wife (Matthew 1:24). If we suppose this happened in Mary's fourth month of pregnancy, it leaves them five months to prepare for their move, travel the three-day journey to Bethlehem, and establish themselves there with months to spare.

> Then, "while they were there, the time came for [Mary] to give birth" (Luke 2:6 ESV).

Matthew and Luke paint Joseph as a considerate man who acted immediately once he received angelic direction. We have every reason to suppose he continued to be considerate and swift in his actions in their move to Bethlehem.

Did Bethlehem reject Mary and Joseph or welcome them?

In many telling's of the Christmas story, Mary and Joseph are turned away from inn after inn, with every house in town rejecting them. Their only recourse is to turn to a dirty stable.

Yet we must remember: this happened in the Middle East, where the locals prize hospitality as one of the highest virtues. It would be unthinkable for a Middle Eastern town to turn away any visitor in need, let alone a pregnant woman. Rejecting a family with a pregnant wife would bring great shame on the entire town.

Further, Bethlehem was Joseph's hometown. His family lineage ran through that town for over a thousand years, all the way back to the time of David. As Kenneth Bailey, a scholarly eminently familiar with ancient Near Eastern customs, states:

> Joseph is of the "house and lineage of David." A recitation of his recent genealogy will open almost any home in Bethlehem. When a self-respecting "son of the village" returns to the town of his origins in the Middle East, a royal welcome always awaits him.[14]

Given these cultural realities, we can have every confidence that Bethlehem welcomed Mary and Joseph. Yet Luke provides another clue, further solidifying the case.

Luke records that Mary visited Elizabeth and Zechariah after the angel visited her. She travels into "the hill country, to a town in Judah," where they lived (Luke 1:39, ESV). To those familiar with the geography of Israel, the meaning jumps out of the page: this is within a few hours' walk of Bethlehem, as Bethlehem is also a town in the hill country of Judah.

This settles the case that Mary and Joseph were well-received in Bethlehem. If they had been rejected by the town, they could simply have walked another few miles and arrived at Elizabeth and Zechariah's doorstep before dinner. They would have welcomed Mary and Joseph eagerly, as they knew full-well who Mary's baby was. They would naturally have provided every accommodation for them.

If Mary and Joseph remained in Bethlehem, even while knowing that a rich welcome stood open to them a few short hours away, it means they enjoyed at least a comparable level of welcome in Bethlehem. The City of David welcomed a descendent of David warmly.

Yet there is one troublesome line left in Luke. He states: "[Mary] laid [Jesus] in a manger, because there was no place for them in the inn" (Luke 2:7, ESV)

How are we to reconcile this line with the cultural demand to care for a family in need? Thus our next question:

Were Mary and Joseph turned away from an inn?

At first blush, it seems obvious that they were. Luke states clearly: "there was no place for them in the inn" (Luke 2:7, ESV)

This word "inn" is the source of our problems. Yet in the language Luke wrote his Gospel, the word does not mean "inn" at all.

The Greek word is *kataluma*. It is a general word that can refer to any kind of lodging place.

There is a precise word that means "inn," yet Luke does not use it in the Christmas story. He employs it instead in the story of the Good Samaritan, who takes the wounded man to an "inn" to care for him. Luke uses the word *pandokheion*, which refers to what we think of as an inn: a building run by an innkeeper who rents rooms out to travelers.

Luke clearly knew that word existed, but he does not use it in the Christmas story. It seems clear that he never meant to convey the idea of an "inn" rejecting Mary and Joseph.

What then does Luke mean when he states that there was no room for Mary and Joseph in the *kataluma*? If this was the only place Luke used this word, we'd be left to wonder. Thankfully, he uses it again, this time clearly describing it:

> [Jesus] said to [the disciples], "Behold, when you have entered the city, a man carrying a jar of water will meet you. Follow him into the house that he enters and tell the master of the house, 'The Teacher says to you, where is the guest room [*kataluma*], where I may eat the Passover with my disciples?' And he will show you a large upper

room furnished; prepare it there." (Luke 22:10–12, ESV)

Luke leaves us no doubt: *kataluma* refers to a guest room in a private residence. In Luke 22, it describes a guest room in a wealthy home, this time built on the upper level of the house. In a rural village like Bethlehem, the guest room could be built onto the side of the house, on its roof, or as a small separate building nearby.

The meaning quickly becomes clear. A local family in Bethlehem indeed received Mary and Joseph, giving them a warm welcome. Yet their guest room was already full, perhaps housing another family who had traveled in for the registration.

Because the guest room was full, the host family welcomed Mary and Joseph into their own living space, the main room of their house.

But here you may ask: why would you say that Mary and Joseph were in a house? Luke says they laid Jesus in a manger. Why would there be a manger in a house?

The answer is that *every* rural home in Israel had mangers inside of it. Israel had few detached stables as we imagine today, a separate building used exclusively for animals. No one wanted such a thing. It left the animals vulnerable to theft at night, as well as leaving them out to shiver in the cold.

In Israel, heat was precious. Wood was relatively scarce and oil was expensive. To heat your home at night, no rural family would set a fire. Instead, they'd bring their animals inside the house. The animals' body heat would raise the temperature inside the home considerably.

Israelites built their homes to accommodate this. A one-room house in the time of Jesus looked roughly like this:

View from above

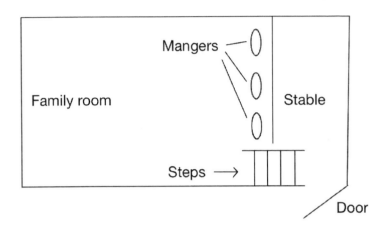

Family room — Mangers — Stable — Steps → — Door

View from the side

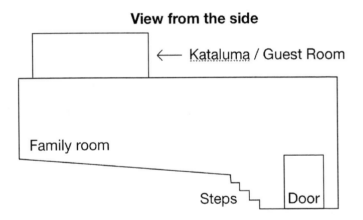

← Kataluma / Guest Room — Family room — Steps — Door

Every evening, the family would bring their animals (a few sheep, a cow, a goat or two) into the stable and close the door. They were therefore safe from theft, while also providing heat to the home.

The family slept the night in the family room, the same room in which they ate their meals and did all the daily activities of living.

On the lip of the family room floor, just before the stable, several mangers were carved into the stone. The family would stock these mangers with hay when the brought the animals in. During the night, if the animals grew hungry, they could grab a quick snack from the manger and go right back to sleep without waking up the family.

In the morning, the family would open the door and let the animals out. They'd clean the house, beginning by sweeping the family room's dust down into the stable. They would then clean out the stable of any animal droppings and move on with the business of the day.

When Luke wrote his Gospel, every person in his audience would understand this instinctively. They all lived in this same style of home. They all accomplished these same chores daily.

When they heard that Mary laid the baby Jesus in a manger, they knew without being told: she was inside the main living room of a family home. The stone manger served as a perfect cradle for the baby, its gently-sloping walls kept the child secure, while the swaddling clothes kept the child warm against the coolness of the stone.

If we don't understand the culture of the region, we assume "manger" means that Mary and Joseph were shunned to a dirty stable away from any other people.

But when we know the culture, "manger" means exactly the opposite. It means their host so eagerly helped the family that they welcomed Joseph and Mary into their own living space, essentially making them "part of the family."

When Mary gave birth, every woman in the host family would be there to assist her, as well as Joseph's nearby relatives. They cared for their children as zealously as we do for ours, if not more so. Middle Eastern hospitality demanded nothing less.

Did the shepherds approve of the conditions Mary, Joseph, and Jesus were living in?

Luke provides one final clue to the hospitable conditions Mary, Joseph, and Jesus found themselves in.

After receiving a startling angelic visit announcing the birth of Jesus:

> [...] the shepherds said to one another, "Let us go over to Bethlehem and see this thing that has happened, which the Lord has made known to us." And they went with haste and found Mary and Joseph, and the baby lying in a manger. [...] And

> the shepherds returned, glorifying and praising God for all they had heard and seen, as it had been told them. (Luke 2:15-16, 20 ESV)

The shepherds found Jesus lying in a manger, which again signifies they found Him inside a village home. The shepherds rejoiced at this and celebrated His birth with Mary, Joseph, and the host family.

Imagine what they would have done if they found Jesus in a drafty outdoor stable. Immediately they would have invited Mary, Joseph, and Jesus into their own homes! The angels just announced the identity of this child: He is "Christ the Lord!" (Luke 2:11 ESV).

Would anyone leave a royal baby in a drafty outdoor stable when they could welcome Him into their own home? Of course not! The shepherds would be jumping over each other to open their own home to host their Messiah.

The reason they didn't do this is clear: they found Jesus already living in acceptable accommodations. The host family was doing such a good job caring for Mary, Joseph, and Jesus that the shepherds didn't feel they could improve on it. Rather, they were "glorifying and praising God for all they had heard and seen" (Luke 2:20).

Meaning Restored

To some, restoring these details won't be terribly significant. They exulted Christ in their hearts at Christmas time already; they will continue to do so, whether Jesus was born in a stable or the family room of a house. And that is a fine attitude to take.

But to others, getting these details right matters. It clears away a lot of incorrect assumptions, many of which made it hard to believe the Christmas story.

Clearing away these misconceptions restores Joseph to a man of consideration and capability. It restores Bethlehem to a hospitable village that cares for those in need. It restores Mary to a warm, welcoming home in which she gives birth with plenty of help. It restores Jesus to being welcomed in a gaggle of eager arms, all excited to hold the baby, their Messiah, their God who has taken on flesh. It restores the shepherds to those who celebrate with the family, increasing their joy, rather than leaving them to shiver in a drafty stable alone. It restores the Christmas story to one whose details make sense to the skeptical reader.

Clearing away these misconceptions also gives our faith a firm foundation, the solid confidence that the events we believe truly happened in history.

Once we grasp the culture that Jesus was born into, the details in Matthew and Luke's accounts snap into place. It is a thoroughly Israeli story, capturing the nuances of first-century Ancient Near-Eastern culture. It therefore bears every mark for authenticity — exactly as we'd expect if Matthew and Luke strove to record the events accurately.

History therefore becomes one of our greatest allies in our continuing quest for Christmas.

Challenge Seven:
Christmas Was Originally a Pagan Holiday

One oft-repeated challenge to Christmas states that Christianity borrowed the celebration from pagan religions that came before. Many religions and cultures celebrated feasts around the time of Christmas, providing plentiful material for the early Church to draw from.

As one magazine opined:

> Christian missionaries adopted Yule celebrations in order to appease and convert pagans who were deeply, spiritually attached to their own holidays. Early Christians were also fascinated by the rural, rustic pagan traditions. [...] The two most notable pagan winter holidays were Germanic Yule and Roman Saturnalia. Christian missionaries gave these holidays a makeover and they are now known to us as Christmas.[15]

What, then, are we to think? Is Christmas merely a reworking of pagan holidays? Are Christians unknowingly engaging in pagan practices every time they celebrate Christmas? Must faithful Christians therefore reject Christmas?

Let's turn to the evidence to find out.

Time to party

To begin with, let's state the obvious: people like celebrating. Our calendars are full of festivals, holidays, and celebrations. The ancient people partied no less.

Whenever Jesus chose to enter the world, there would be a celebration nearby on the calendar.

Winter, in particular, provides several reasons for celebration. The winter solstice occurs on December 21st, the time at which the days stop getting shorter and start getting longer. That's reason alone to celebrate. The cold, dark of winter also provides a reason to gather, cheering each other's hearts with light and warmth in the midst of celebration.

Given all this, it is no problem for Christmas that other ancient religions held festivals in the same season. It couldn't be avoided, no matter which season in which Jesus chose to appear.

The question for us, then, is this: Did Christians appropriate the traditions of these prior festivals, or did Christians have another reason — a uniquely *Christian* reason — to celebrate Christ on December 25th?

The wise men lead the way

As we explored in the previous chapter, the wise men followed the Star of Bethlehem — Jupiter — in their quest to find the King who had been born to the Jews. When they looked down to Bethlehem from Jerusalem, they found Jupiter entering retrograde motion, standing still in the sky directly over the city of David.

This happened precisely on December 25th, 2 B.C.

The wise men no doubt raced down to Bethlehem, eager to find the Messiah they had traveled so long to meet. That night they found Jesus and presented Him with their gifts: gold, frankincense, and myrrh. They gave these gifts not only to Jesus, but to His family, as the gold provided the resources they would need to survive their flight to Egypt.

This memory of this first Christmas celebration endured, as Matthew featured it at the beginning of his Gospel. It should be no surprise to us, then, that future generations of Christians chose to commemorate the birth of the Messiah as the wise men did: praising Jesus together on December 25th while giving gifts.

Yet Christmas is celebrated world-wide. Many Christians, particularly those in the Eastern Orthodox and Armenian traditions, celebrate Christmas on January 6th. Why would they celebrate on this date, as opposed to the day the wise men found Jesus?

The answer is remarkably simple: it is the same date.

> When Pope Gregory XIII established the Gregorian calendar in 1582, he ushered in an era in which the people of Europe disagreed on what day it was. As a result, they celebrated Christmas on different days. Before the Gregorian reform Europe had adhered to the Julian calendar, which was a full ten days behind the newly instituted Gregorian calendar. Some nations and churches refused to adopt the Gregorian reforms. In these lands people continued to celebrate Christmas on December 25, but did so according to the Julian calendar. Their celebrations fell on January 5 according to the new Gregorian calendar. In past eras the English sometimes referred to January 5 or 6 as "Old Christmas Day."[16]

The difference is therefore not one of the date, but rather the calendar used to find the date. Whether we celebrate this year on December 25th or January 6th, we are continuing in the tradition of the wise men who celebrated Jesus.

The forest or the trees

This might exonerate the date, but what of the festivities? Many of our traditional Christmas decorations supposedly descend from pagan influences. As one researcher claims:

> Another custom we can thank the pagans for? Christmas trees. Davis explained that the evergreen trees signaled the "return of life" and "light" as the winter solstice meant the days were starting to get longer. "They started to hang an apple on it, so little red balls on green trees — get the picture here?"[17]

Should Christians therefore toss our Christmas trees out on the snow, never to shed a pine needle on our living rooms again?

The evidence suggests otherwise. Long before pagans began hanging apples on pine trees, God commissioned evergreen trees to sing His praises:

> Praise the LORD!
> Praise the LORD from the heavens;
> praise him in the heights!
> Praise him, all his angels;
> praise him, all his hosts! [...]
>
> Praise the LORD from the earth,
> you great sea creatures and all deeps,
> fire and hail, snow and mist,

> stormy wind fulfilling his word!
> Mountains and all hills,
> fruit trees and *all cedars!*
>
> […] Let them praise the name of the LORD,
> for his name alone is exalted;
> his majesty is above earth and heaven.
> (Psalm 148:1-2, 7-9, 13 ESV, emphasis added)

God also employs pine trees as signs of His goodness to His people:

> "For you shall go out in joy
> and be led forth in peace;
> the mountains and the hills before you
> shall break forth into singing,
> and *all the trees of the field shall clap their hands.*
> Instead of the thorn shall come up the *cypress*;
> instead of the brier shall come up the myrtle;
> and it shall make a name for the LORD,
> an everlasting sign that shall not be cut off." (Isaiah 55:12–13 ESV)

If God can utilize pine trees to praise His name and signify His goodness, then Christians have all the right in the world to place one of these trees inside their homes on the day when they celebrate this very same God.

Kindness is king

87

Scripture may indeed give us full warrant to celebrate Christmas with all our favorite decorations and traditions.

But let us always remember the heart of Christmas: *love*.

If a fellow Christian (or a neighbor from another faith tradition) struggles with these ideas, there's no need to force Christmas celebrations upon them. As Paul states:

> "Be careful, however, that the exercise of your rights does not become a stumbling block to the weak" (1 Corinthians 8:9 NIV).

May we never celebrate Christmas in a way that causes someone to stumble. Let us instead remember Christ, who gave up His rights to take on flesh, loving us by living among us. If He can give His rights up to love us, so can we give up our rights to love each other.

But what if we're wrong?

For the sake of argument, let's suppose that tomorrow archaeologists dig up an ancient parchment from an early church leader. Suppose this leader states directly: "We will take the pagan holiday Saturnalia and transform it into a Christian holiday." What would we think then? Would we need to discard Christmas?

No more so than Paul needed to discard pagan poetry on Mars Hill.

Acts 17 records one of the greatest evangelistic messages of all time. In Athens, Greece, the Apostle Paul presented the good news of Jesus Christ to a Gentile audience, one who knew nothing of Judaism or the Bible.

Instead of appealing to the Bible, Paul appealed to things the Greeks already knew. He appealed to one of their own religious altars and their own poets. He did so openly and boldly:

> So Paul, standing in the midst of the Areopagus, said:
>
> "Men of Athens, I perceive that in every way you are very religious. For as I passed along and observed the objects of your worship, I found also an altar with this inscription: 'To the unknown god.' What therefore you worship as unknown, this I proclaim to you.
>
> The God who made the world and everything in it, being Lord of heaven and earth, does not live in temples made by man, nor is he served by human hands, as though he needed anything, since he himself gives to all mankind life and breath and everything.
>
> And he made from one man every nation of mankind to live on all the face of the earth, having determined allotted periods and the boundaries of

> their dwelling place, that they should seek God, and perhaps feel their way toward him and find him. Yet he is actually not far from each one of us, for
>
> "'In him we live and move and have our being';
> as even some of your own poets have said,
> "'For we are indeed his offspring.' (Acts 17:22–28, ESV)

If Paul can appropriate pagan religious altars and pagan poetry to communicate the good news of Jesus, then Christians should have no trouble whatsoever appropriating a feast to celebrate the birth of Jesus.

After all, God has written the clues of His existence throughout the world. People of every culture pick up on them, to some extent. Christians can therefore follow Paul's example in picking up on these threads and following them back to their origin: the God of Heaven who loves us so deeply that He took on flesh to live among us, and then to die for us.

We can celebrate this God every day of the year.

We can worship this Jesus every moment of our lives.

And we can certainly praise Him together on December 25th (or January 6th).

Challenge Eight:
Matthew Invented the Bethlehem Massacre

Out of all the aspects of the Christmas story, the Bethlehem massacre is the one we would most like to forget.

It is a horrible story, one seldom presented in all our Christmas movies and plays. No one wants to remember such a horror on the day when we want most of all to feel peace, hope, and love.

Yet Matthew includes this tragedy in his account of Christmas, and so we must wrestle with it. We must grapple with why he includes it — yet no one else even mentions it.

At the conclusion of his Christmas story, Matthew relates the following:

> Now when [the wise men] had departed, behold, an angel of the Lord appeared to Joseph in a dream

91

and said, "Rise, take the child and his mother, and flee to Egypt, and remain there until I tell you, for Herod is about to search for the child, to destroy him."

And he rose and took the child and his mother by night and departed to Egypt and remained there until the death of Herod. This was to fulfill what the Lord had spoken by the prophet, "Out of Egypt I called my son."

Then Herod, when he saw that he had been tricked by the wise men, became furious, and he sent and killed all the male children in Bethlehem and in all that region who were two years old or under, according to the time that he had ascertained from the wise men. Then was fulfilled what was spoken by the prophet Jeremiah:

> "A voice was heard in Ramah,
>   weeping and loud lamentation,
> Rachel weeping for her children;
>   she refused to be comforted, because they are no more." (Matthew 2:13-18 ESV)

This is a story we'd like to forget. Many scholars tell us that we *should* forget it — that Matthew invented everything about it. One such scholar notes:

> This episode is not mentioned in any sources aside from the Gospel of Matthew [...] This means there is no independent confirmation that this event ever occurred. Furthermore, Herod's command echoes Pharaoh's order to have all first-born Hebrew males put to death (Exodus 1:22), thereby presenting Jesus as a new Moses. [...] For these reasons, many scholars believe that the massacre of the innocents never occurred, but instead was inspired by Herod's reputation for executing his own sons.[18]

In our quest for Christmas, we face two challenges: why Matthew included this story, and why no one else does.

Let's tackle the second challenge first.

Could Herod have done such a thing?

Regardless of their opinion of the massacre itself, historians have no trouble whatsoever believing that Herod was capable of such an atrocity.

Herod began his reign nearly noble but died a madman with the blood of countless souls on his hands. Near the end of his life, where Matthew records the Bethlehem massacre happening, Herod viewed any potential rival as a threat to be neutralized immediately. Herod executed three of his own sons — Antipater, Alexander, and

93

Aristobulus — out of the paranoid belief that they wanted to steal his throne. This brutality prompted Caesar Augustus to remark, "It is better to be Herod's pig than son."[19] The pig would live longer.

Perhaps the worst example of Herod's cruelty occurred as he lay dying. He knew that his death would not be mourned by Israel, given how horrifically he had treated the common people. Yet Herod wanted people to mourn when he died. He ordered thousands of prominent men from Israel to assemble in Jericho, under penalty of death. Then Herod ordered that as soon as he died, his soldiers were to slaughter all the men who had gathered. His hoped that every family in Israel would lose a loved one, guaranteeing the nation would mourn on the day Herod passed. Mercifully, his soldiers refused the order.[20]

If such a man could execute his own sons and thousands of innocent men, it is no stretch to imagine that he could order the death of all the male babies in Bethlehem — particularly if he feared one of them would try to steal his throne.

Did the massacre happen?

Given Herod's brutality and the detailed record provided by Matthew, it is nearly certain that the massacre did occur.

Many scholars take issue with this conclusion, arguing
that because no one else mentions the massacre, it's likely
Matthew made it up. As Jodi Magness stated above,
scholars suppose that Matthew wanted to juice up Jesus'
story to sound more like Moses'. Matthew therefore
invented the massacre to parallel Pharaoh's slaughter of
all Hebrew male infants.

Yet all this skepticism ignores a critical issue: anyone who
wanted to verify the details of the massacre could go and
check.

Matthew wrote his Gospel to a predominantly Jewish
audience. History records that Matthew published his
Gospel while Peter and Paul were still alive.[21] Plentiful
eyewitnesses still lived who could testify to the contents
of the Gospel.

Memories were long in Israel. If anyone read Matthew's
Gospel, then traveled to Bethlehem to verify the story,
everyone in town would remember it.

Who forgets the murder of their child? If Herod indeed
killed all the male children two years and under, nearly
every family would have lost a son. They would
remember. Their children would remember. Their
grandchildren would remember. The story would be
passed down, honoring the memory of those who died,
and reminding every generation not to trust Rome.

Bethlehem lay a mere five miles from Jerusalem, the center of all religious and cultural life in Israel. Every faithful Israelite traveled up to Jerusalem several times a year to celebrate the feasts. This afforded every traveler the opportunity to stop by Bethlehem and verify Matthew's story.

Lies versus truth

When liars craft their fables, they try to make the lies as undetectable as possible. Liars don't want to be found out. They will carefully select the details in their stories to be as hard to verify as possible, giving their lies the greatest chance of being believed.

Matthew does the opposite.

If Matthew wanted to fabricate a story to bolster Jesus' birth narrative, this is the opposite of how he'd do it. If the Bethlehem massacre was a lie, everyone could disprove it by taking a small detour on their next trip to Jerusalem. If they found it false, and word got around, it would destroy the credibility of his Gospel.

If Matthew wanted to invent a story, he'd try to make it as hard to disprove as possible. Such a lie is easy to conceive: perhaps Herod realized Jesus slipped through his fingers. Instead of trying to kill any potential child-king in Bethlehem, Herod could order a dozen children randomly executed throughout the land, out of vengeance. This would spread out the lie, such that if no eyewitnesses could be found — well, the executions were random and well spread-out, so it's no surprise it's hard to find them. Such a lie would give Matthew's story plausible cover.

Yet Matthew doesn't make any attempt to hide his story. He makes as bold and public a claim as possible, with every opportunity given to prove him wrong.

History doesn't record the first hint that anyone ever doubted Matthew's account. Powerful enemies surrounded Christianity for the first three hundred years of its existence. They seized every opportunity to try to attack this new faith that followed Jesus. Yet not a single opponent ever dared to call Matthew a liar.

Given this reality, we have every reason to believe this massacre truly happened.

But why remember it?

Even if this event is historical, Matthew did not have to include it. Jesus lived a dynamic life full of adventure. Surely Matthew could have selected a more positive story from Jesus' life and skipped the horror!

Yet Matthew not only includes the story, but uses it as a somber crescendo to his entire Christmas narrative.

Why did he do so? Why include tragedy at Christmas?

The answer is that tragedy finds us at every stage in life. Tragedy hits hard whenever it strikes, yet it burns hottest in times when everyone else feels joy — like Christmas.

Matthew reminds us — vividly, painfully, unavoidably — that Jesus did not enter a perfect world. Jesus entered a world in pain, a world where the powerful terrorize the weak, a world where Rachel weeps for her children.

This is a world that needs a Savior.

This is a Savior who is reminded — every time He hears the story of His own birth — that this world desperately needs rescue.

Is sin real? Does sin matter?

Every drop of blood in Bethlehem proves it does. This is a world gripped by sin, a world where pride, anger, power, lust, and greed rule unquestioned. Sin is not a quaint spiritual idea, but the driving force behind every ounce of pain we endure.

Sin lies at the heart of every problem we encounter. Sin is the darkness clouding the world, dividing us from each other, hiding us from God, separating us from the joy, love, and peace we all crave.

Sin is the darkness into which this Savior dares to shine:

The true light, which gives light to everyone, was coming into the world. He was in the world, and the world was made through him, yet the world did not know him. He came to his own, and his own people did not receive him. But to all who did receive him, who believed in his name, he gave the right to become children of God, who were born, not of blood nor of the will of the flesh nor of the will of man, but of God. (John 1:9–13, ESV)

Challenge Nine:
A Virgin Birth Is Impossible

To those outside the church, the virgin birth is often the first stumbling block that sends them reeling.

If you've been in church all your life, you barely notice the virgin birth at Christmas. It's so familiar it goes by almost without notice.

But if you've never heard the Christmas story before, the idea that a woman could give birth without a human father is ludicrous.

Who could believe such a thing in a modern day and age? We know how babies form. Embryos require the DNA of a mother *and* father. Women can't give birth to a baby with only her own DNA, and a woman certainly can't give birth to a *male* child with only the mother's female DNA to work with. To be male, the child needs a Y chromosome, but the mother would have only two X chromosomes.

Summarizing the thoughts of many modern thinkers, Gerd Lüdemann states:

> First however a firm line must be drawn. The statement that Jesus was engendered by the Spirit and born of a virgin is a falsification of the historical facts. At all events he had a human father. From this it follows first that any interpretation which fails to take a clear stand here is to be branded a lie.[22]

Why, then, do Matthew and Luke speak so certainly of a virgin birth? Does this stand as a mark against the authenticity of the Christmas story, as they hinge its truth on a scientific impossibility?

Or to say it another way: must we abandon scientific truth to cling to theological truth?

A clearly impossible birth

Despite the clear realities of how conception works, Luke dares to tell us that God worked another way. He writes:

> In the sixth month the angel Gabriel was sent from God to a city of Galilee named Nazareth, to a virgin betrothed to a man whose name was Joseph, of the house of David. And the virgin's name was Mary. And he came to her and said, "Greetings, O favored one, the Lord is with you! [...] And behold, you

> will conceive in your womb and bear a son, and you shall call his name Jesus." [...]
>
> And Mary said to the angel, "How will this be, since I am a virgin?"
>
> And the angel answered her, "The Holy Spirit will come upon you, and the power of the Most High will overshadow you; therefore the child to be born will be called holy—the Son of God."
>
> And Mary said, "Behold, I am the servant of the Lord; let it be to me according to your word." And the angel departed from her. (Luke 1:26-28, 31, 34-35, ESV)

Mary understands that conception requires both parents. Some skeptics have claimed that people in the ancient world didn't know any better, and would easily accept the idea of a virgin birth. Yet Luke's account states otherwise. Mary herself is skeptical of the idea, seeing it as flatly impossible.

Joseph, likewise, is convinced that Mary's pregnancy resulted from her being unfaithful to him. It takes a full-out angelic visit to convince him that the baby truly is from God (Matthew 1:18-25). If Mary and Joseph never considered a virgin birth to be physically possible, no one else in the ancient world did, either.

A virgin birth is flatly impossible.

Unless God gets involved.

How the impossible happened

As scientists began grasping the fundamentals of human genetics, a virgin birth seemed impossible. Gender results from a different pair of chromosomes. Women possess two X chromosomes, while males require an XY chromosome. No mother, no matter how pious she may be, contains the Y chromosome necessary for her child to be a male. For that, she needs a father.

Yet as we learned more and more, a virgin birth began to make sense. More than that, it became *possible.*

Through in vitro fertilization, a woman can give birth to a baby whose father she has never slept with. Doctors can place an embryo in the uterus of a woman, even a virgin woman, who can then carry the baby to term and give birth to a healthy child — even a male child.

To be sure, if God exists, He can do whatever miracle He pleases. Omnipotence grants Him such a right.

Yet it is just like God to hide the secrets of human genetics in plain sight. If Mary became pregnant by the Holy Spirit, as Gabriel declared, we can reasonably well understand how it happened. The Holy Spirit placed Jesus as an embryo inside Mary's uterus, where the embryo implanted and began growing. Mary could indeed carry and give birth to a male child, completely independent of a human father. Generations ago, it would have seemed fanciful. Today, it's science.

To ask someone to believe in the virgin birth, we're only asking them to believe in what modern science can replicate. God, who designed humanity and created every one of us, performs the same work that a doctor can perform today.

Why it was necessary

On one hand, the virgin birth seems a bit unnecessary.

Throughout the Old Testament, God shows up frequently in flesh. We call these appearances Theophanies, or to some, Christophanies — Christ appearing before His birth.

In Genesis 32, Jacob wrestles with a man all night — a messenger from God. This mysterious visitor and Jacob himself both identify this man as God. The man himself says to Jacob, "Your name shall no longer be called Jacob, but Israel, for you have striven with God and with men, and have prevailed" (Genesis 32:28, ESV). After the visitor left, Jacob "called the name of the place Peniel, saying 'For I have seen God face-to-face, and yet my life has been delivered'" (Genesis 32:30, ESV).

Several hundred years later, Moses and the elders of Israel witness this same God face-to-face:

> Then Moses and Aaron, Nadab, and Abihu, and seventy of the elders of Israel went up, and *they saw the God of Israel*. There was under his feet as it were a pavement of sapphire stone, like the very heaven for clearness. And he did not lay his hand on the chief men of the people of Israel; they beheld God, and ate and drank. (Exodus 24:9–11, ESV, emphasis added)

Moses beheld God who stood before him in a body, standing on His own feet on a pavement of sapphire stone. There is no doubt that this is the God of Israel, that He has a body, and that He is appearing to His people.

If Jesus can therefore appear without being born, why did He need to be born of Mary at Christmas? Why could Jesus not simply appear as He had before and carry out His Messianic work?

The answer is simply this: Jesus needed a human parent because Jesus needed to become a genuine human being, and genuine human beings need parents.

The Apostle Paul pealed the veil back from Jesus' virgin birth, telling the story of how God came from Heaven to earth:

> Have this mind among yourselves, which is yours in Christ Jesus, who, though he was in the form of God, did not count equality with God a thing to be grasped, but emptied himself, by taking the form of a servant, being born in the likeness of men. (Philippians 2:5–7, ESV)

Jesus dwelt in eternity as God. Yet He did not grasp onto His divinity, refusing to let it go. Rather, He chose to empty Himself of His divine attributes. He chose to limit Himself into genuine human form, the form of a servant, the likeness of humanity.

Jesus did not cease being God, but rather set His divine abilities aside. You can do the same. A person who can see can choose to empty themselves of that ability. They can close their eyes. With eyes closed, they now experience life as the blind do. They still possess the ability to see, in much the same way that Jesus still retained all His divine abilities. But by choice, these abilities are set aside, in order to enter into the kind of life that another lives.

Jesus did this for one clear reason:

> And being found in human form, he humbled himself by becoming obedient to the point of death, even death on a cross. (Philippians 2:8 ESV)

Jesus came to die the death that we were meant to die.

For that, Jesus had to be *able* to die.

Jesus emptied Himself down into the genuine limitations of humanity. If His body was killed, He would die, as any human would. He had to do this to accomplish His purpose:

> Since therefore the children share in flesh and blood, he himself likewise partook of the same things, that through death he might destroy the one who has the power of death, that is, the devil, and deliver all those who through fear of death were subject to lifelong slavery. [...] Therefore he had to be made like his brothers in every respect, so that he might become a merciful and faithful high priest in the service of God, to make propitiation for the sins of the people. (Hebrews 2:14–17, ESV)

Why did Jesus have to be born of a virgin at Christmas?

Because Jesus had to die.

He had to die to atone for the sins of His people — to die the death that we deserved to die, so that in Him, we could truly live. As Paul again declared:

> For God made Christ, who never sinned, to be the offering for our sin, so that we could be made right with God through Christ. (2 Corinthians 5:21).

Christmas is a time of giving. In Christ, God gave Himself

to the world. Through the death of Christ, God gave life to everyone, so that "everyone who calls on the name of the LORD will be saved" (Romans 10:13, Joel 2:32, Acts 2:21).

In this way, Christmas truly is a time for:

> Glory to God in the highest heaven, and on earth peace to those on whom his favor rests. (Luke 2:14, ESV)

God's peace rests on those who call on His Name. The ones who choose to trust in Him — these are the people He favors.

This Christmastime salvation therefore brings all glory to God. Jesus submitted Himself to death, saving humanity. Therefore:

> God has highly exalted him and bestowed on him the name that is above every name, so that at the name of Jesus every knee should bow, in heaven and on earth and under the earth, and every tongue confess that Jesus Christ is Lord, to the glory of God the Father. (Philippians 2:9–11, ESV)

Challenge Ten: The "Immanuel" Prophecy Wasn't Meant for Jesus

If you've attended church at Christmastime, you've likely heard Isaiah 7:14 read aloud. The Gospel of Matthew features it prominently in the Christmas story:

> All this took place to fulfill what the Lord had spoken by the prophet:
>> "Behold, the virgin [*almah*] shall conceive and bear a son,
>> and they shall call his name Immanuel"
>> (which means, God with us). (Matthew 1:22–23 ESV)

It's a simple, beautiful, accurate prophecy of Jesus, made hundreds of years before His birth.

Or is it?

Prominent scholars say it isn't. They argue that the prophecy of Isaiah 7:14 had nothing to do with Jesus, but rather focused on events 700 years before Jesus appeared:

> Numerous identifications of Immanuel have been proposed, the most important of which are a royal child of the Davidic line, often identified specifically as Hezekiah, or a son of the prophet Isaiah [Maher-shalal-hash-baz]. [...] Because the identity of the *almâ* is never made clear, it is impossible to identify Immanuel with certainty.[23]

In this light, the Immanuel prophecy seems doomed to confusion and mystery. Worse, if the prophecy has no way to know who it's referring to, then Christians are grasping at straws to try to force the prophecy to apply to Jesus.

Yet God does not give prophecy to be confusing. Prophecy must contain clear markers by which to identify its fulfillment, or else it cannot fulfill its purpose.

Can we therefore identify clear markers in the prophecy, then examine them against the three main candidates?

Indeed we can.

God wanted us to.

A precise prophecy

Let's a closer look at the verse:

> Therefore the Lord himself will give you a sign. Behold, the virgin [almah] shall conceive and bear a son, and shall call his name Immanuel. (Isaiah 7:14 ESV)

Focus your attention on two key criteria:

- A virgin ("*almah*" in Hebrew) will conceive a child

- The baby is called Immanuel

"*Almah*" always referred to a maiden, an unmarried woman of sterling character, chaste and pure. Every *almah* is a virgin because the Hebrew culture praised and protected virginity highly. In Jewish culture, any young woman of marriageable age would be understood to be a virgin.

God gives this prophecy as a sign—which means it must be unique, unusual, or bizarre. It must stand out as unusual, or it can't function as a sign.

A virgin giving birth would certainly qualify. But a married woman conceiving and birthing would not. It's too normal to be a sign.

Let's compare these two criteria to the three main candidates: Maher-shalal-hash-baz, Hezekiah, and Jesus.

111

Maher-shalal-hash-baz

First, let's look at the child who comes in Chapter 8. Given that the birth of Immanuel is prophesied in Chapter 7, and Maher-shalal-has-baz is born in Chapter 8, many have assumed he fulfills the prophecy:

> And I went to the prophetess, and she conceived and bore a son. Then the LORD said to me, "Call his name Maher-shalal-hash-baz" (Isaiah 8:3 ESV)

The proximity to the prophecy seems to be the only mark in Maher-shalal-hash-baz' favor. He simply doesn't fit the prophecy:

- A married woman, Isaiah's wife, conceived this child. She already had given birth to one son, Shear-jashub. A married woman who had already given birth is no longer considered an *almah*.

- Maher-shalal-hash-baz is never called "Immanuel," but is given a different name entirely, meaning "The spoil speeds, the prey hastens."

Maher-shalal-hash-baz is out of contention. How about the next popular option?

Hezekiah

Hezekiah is harder to judge, as his birth is not narrated. Yet this in itself argues against Hezekiah being the fulfillment, since the prophesy is given deliberately as a sign. Scripture would not emphasize the sign, then ignore its fulfillment!

Additionally, Hezekiah was already alive at the time the prophecy was given. That makes it impossible that his birth could be a divine and miraculous sign for the future, because it had already happened.

We can therefore determine the answers to our criteria:

- Hezekiah's mother was married, therefore not an *almah*.

- Hezekiah is not called Immanuel anywhere in Scripture, nor is his life called out in any significant way to signify that God is with us.

These two options are out. What of the third option – the one we sing about at Christmas?

Jesus

How does Jesus compare to Hezekiah and Maher-shalal-hash-baz? Matthew provides all the detail we need:

> Now the birth of Jesus Christ took place in this way. When his mother Mary had been betrothed to Joseph, before they came together she was found to be with child from the Holy Spirit.
>
> An angel of the Lord appeared to him in a dream, saying, "Joseph, son of David, do not fear to take Mary as your wife, for that which is conceived in her is from the Holy Spirit. She will bear a son, and you shall call his name Jesus, for he will save his people from their sins."
>
> All this took place to fulfill what the Lord had spoken by the prophet: "Behold, the virgin shall conceive and bear a son, and they shall call his name Immanuel" (which means, God with us). (Matthew 1:18, 20-23 ESV)

We have our two details met:

- Mary conceives while a virgin, something impossible unless God causes it to happen — which is the point. It's unique, making it a powerful sign.

- The name "Jesus" fulfills the meaning of "Immanuel" directly.

To see this second criterion clearly, all we need to do is spell out what each name means:

- "Immanuel" in Hebrew means "God with us."

- "Jesus" means "God saves."

Now look again at what the angel says:

"You shall call his name Jesus, for he will save his people from their sins."

When you read this in the original languages, the meaning screams out at you. You shall call his name "God saves," for he will save his people from their sins.

Every time people used the name "Jesus," they declared the truth of Immanuel — God is with us.

Good news of great joy — 700 years of it

God never gives prophecy without a reason. Typically, He weaves depths of meaning into each prophecy that yield greater treasures the deeper we dig.

The Immanuel prophecy indeed points to Jesus, yet those who heard it didn't have to wait 700 years for Jesus to arrive before they could appreciate what it meant. God gave this prophecy amid one of the most terrifying events in Israel's history:

In the days of Ahaz the son of Jotham, son of Uzziah, king of Judah, Rezin the king of Syria and Pekah the son of Remaliah the king of Israel came up to Jerusalem to wage war against it, but could not yet mount an attack against it. When the house of David was told, "Syria is in league with Ephraim," the heart of Ahaz and the heart of his people shook as the trees of the forest shake before the wind. [...]

Again the LORD spoke to Ahaz: "Ask a sign of the LORD your God; let it be deep as Sheol or high as heaven."

But Ahaz said, "I will not ask, and I will not put the LORD to the test."

And he said, "Hear then, O house of David! Is it too little for you to weary men, that you weary my God also? Therefore the Lord himself will give you a sign. Behold, the virgin shall conceive and bear a son, and shall call his name Immanuel. He shall eat curds and honey when he knows how to refuse the evil and choose the good. For before the boy knows how to refuse the evil and choose the good, the land whose two kings you dread will be deserted. (Isaiah 7:1-2, 10-16, ESV)

Amid an invasion threatening to destroy Ahaz' entire

country, God offers Ahaz a sign. When he refuses, God gives him one, and a far better sign that Ahaz could ever have hoped to ask for.

God promises the coming of Immanuel — God with us. This is the good news of Christmas, the story we celebrate every year.

Yet Ahaz probably cared far more about the next two lines.

Immanuel will be a remarkable child. He'll know how to refuse evil and choose good when he is eating curds and honey. These are early child foods, some of the earliest solid foods a child will transition to. Yet even at this incredibly young age, the child will be able to discern between good and evil.

Yet before this Immanuel child learns discernment, the object of Ahaz' terror will be destroyed. Ahaz shook like a tree caught in a windstorm when he heard that the kings of Syria and the northern ten tribes of Israel marched on Jerusalem.

In this prophecy, God declared to Ahaz in no uncertain terms: your kingdom will outlast theirs.

One day there will come a child so remarkable that he will discern good and evil when he's still eating the food of early childhood. This child will be born of an *almah*, an event so unusual that it will serve as a supernatural sign to all who have ears to hear.

117

When this child arrives, your kingdom will still endure. Yet the two kingdoms preparing to attack you will have fallen, their lands deserted.

Ahaz never lived to see this fulfillment. But to him, that would be exceedingly good news.

The further into the future this prophecy reached, the better the news was for Ahaz. It meant that his kingdom would endure, and his people would survive, however far into the future God prophesied about.

That spoke directly to Ahaz' greatest fear: that these two kings would destroy his people, his land, and his own life. God assured Ahaz that his people would endure, far past those who sought to wipe them out.

A clear prophecy for a clear purpose

Skeptics of the Bible will often claim that its prophecies are vague and nebulous, written loosely so that they can apply to almost anything.

But the Immanuel prophecy isn't vague in the slightest.

It has a clear *sign* — a virgin giving birth.

It has a clear *focus* — a child, Immanuel, "God with us," who will mature to moral wisdom far more swiftly than most children.

118

It has a clear *promise* — before this child learns moral discernment, the lands of the two kings Ahaz dreads will be deserted.

It has a clear *hope* — the people of God will long outlive these two enemies.

It has a clear *intent* — to reassure the people of God that He will save them.

God fulfilled every aspect of this prophecy, down to the last letter.

At Christmas, God appeared among us. Everyone who heard of His appearance could think back to Isaiah's prophecy and reflect on God's abundant faithfulness.

God had indeed preserved His people over 700 years of hardship. God had indeed protected His people, such that they could receive the Christ child at Christmas, while their enemies had long since suffered defeat.

In the Immanuel prophecy, God put Himself on display as a Savior who can deliver His people from the worst fates. When Jesus appeared and took on the title Immanuel, it carried 700 years of fulfilled promise.

God indeed saves, exactly as He promised.

God indeed loves, rescuing His people from their fears.

God indeed cares, taking His people's burdens on Himself.

This is the great joy of Christmas: this amazing God is with us.

Challenge Eleven:
The Gospels Invented Jesus Fulfilling Prophecy After the Fact

Prophecy is supposed to astound us.

It is a calling card unique to the God of the Bible. Alone out of all the world's holy books, the Bible packs its pages with prophecy, constantly telling the future in precise detail. It's meant to amaze us.

Matthew and Luke fill their Christmas accounts with fulfilled prophecy. They declare boldly that Jesus is the long-prophesied Messiah, proving it by all the Messianic prophecies that Jesus — and only Jesus — fulfilled.

But in order to be amazed by prophecy, we need the certainty that Jesus truly fulfilled them. As readers, we come to these prophecies long after their fulfillment. We're trusting the word of Matthew and Luke that Jesus really fulfilled these ancient prophecies.

121

How do we know that Matthew and Luke didn't invent these fulfillments after the fact? If they wanted to impress their audiences, perhaps they could pick a few prophecies from the Old Testament and invent a New Testament fulfillment for them. If they knew the prophecies everyone expected Messiah to fulfill, it wouldn't be hard to write up a few stories where Jesus just so happened to fulfill them.

In short: how do we know that these fulfillments really happened?

This question might be uncomfortable, but it's crucial. If Jesus never fulfilled the prophecies for being Messiah, then He claims are bunk and no one should follow Him.

But if Jesus truly fulfilled all the dozens of Messianic prophecies — specific prophecies recorded hundreds of years before He was born — then we have evidence of divine work.

So let's get down to it: how do we know for sure that Jesus fulfilled these Christmas prophecies?

We possess three powerful answers.

First: Without fulfilled prophecy, no one would have followed Jesus in the first place.

If anyone claims to be Messiah, faithful followers of God have one primary way to test them: *do they fulfill the prophecies?* The Old Testament provides Israel with dozens of prophecies to measure any Messianic claimant by. They are designed to be specific, so that every false claimant is exposed. We would never read about Jesus if He had failed to fulfill the basic prophecies.

Imagine the scene:

Jesus enters a village and claims to be Messiah. A crowd gathers because every good Jew is yearning for Messiah to appear. Someone from the crowd recites a prophecy from Isaiah, listing one sign of Messiah's coming:

> "At that time the deaf will be able to hear words read from a scroll, and the eyes of the blind will be able to see through deep darkness. The downtrodden will again rejoice in the LORD; the poor among humankind will take delight in the Holy One of Israel" (Isaiah 29:18-19, ESV).

So they say: "Jesus, you claim to be Messiah. Can you heal a deaf person? Can you restore blind eyes?"

Jesus fidgets and mumbles and tries to shift the topic. The crowd soon realizes nothing will happen and goes back to their daily business.

And that would be the end of the story. If you can't do what Messiah must do, then you're not Messiah.

Fulfilled prophecy was Messiah's calling card. Jesus fulfilled every prophecy that Messiah needed to fulfill — in His first coming. Jesus' enemies could find no grounds to dismiss Him as Messiah. Even in their eyes, He fulfilled the prophecies. To try to deny Jesus as Messiah, they resorted to ludicrous claims, such as asserting that Jesus cast out demons by the power of other demons (Matthew 12:24, Luke 11:15).

That's our first sign that Jesus truly fulfilled these prophecies: the only reason we're talking about Jesus is because He did. If He never had, no one would have followed Him, and there would be nothing to discuss.

Second: The prophecies recorded in the Gospels are public. That means they are easily verifiable or falsifiable.

If the Gospel writers were slipping in fake prophetic fulfillment after the fact, you'd expect them to make the details quiet. Liars try to make their lies as undetectable as possible.

But the prophecies Jesus fulfilled are public and grand. They're not what you'd invent if you were trying to hide something fake.

Consider Jesus' birth in Bethlehem, fulfilling the prophecy from Micah, which everyone knew to be a prophecy of the Messiah:

> "And you, Bethlehem, in the land of Judah, are in no way least among the rulers of Judah, for out of you will come a Ruler who will shepherd My people Israel." (Micah 5:2 ESV)

If the Gospel writers wanted to invent a fake birth in Bethlehem, you'd expect them to make it quiet. Perhaps Mary and Joseph stopped in town just to give birth, then immediately got back on the road. They could claim that no locals remember the event because it was so quick that most people missed it.

But the Gospels record the opposite.

The Gospels record a series of unforgettable events. The wise men alone would make for a story passed down by the locals through generations. But the truly unforgettable horror came from Herod, who sent soldiers to slaughter every male child two years old and under. Everyone remembered that atrocity. Who forgets the murder of their child?

This fulfills the prophecy from Jeremiah:

> "A voice was heard in Ramah,
> weeping and loud lamentation,
> Rachel weeping for her children;
> she refused to be comforted,
> because they are no more." (Matthew 2:18;
> Jeremiah 31:15, ESV).

The Gospels record Bethlehem as Joseph's hometown. His family lineage ran through Bethlehem for generations, all the way back to the time of David. This lineage is central to being Messiah, as the core prophecies declared that Messiah would be a descendent of David:

> For to us a child is born,
>> to us a son is given;
> and the government shall be upon his shoulder,
>> and his name shall be called
> Wonderful Counselor, Mighty God,
>> Everlasting Father, Prince of Peace.
> Of the increase of his government and of peace
>> there will be no end,
> on the throne of David and over his kingdom,
>> to establish it and to uphold it
> with justice and with righteousness
>> from this time forth and forevermore.
> The zeal of the LORD of hosts will do this.
> (Isaiah 9:6-7, ESV)

All these prophecies found their fulfillments in Bethlehem. This small village, known as the City of David to the locals, is a mere five miles from Jerusalem, the center of Israel's political and religious life. Every faithful Jew traveled to Jerusalem for the yearly feasts. Anyone who wanted to check the Gospel stories with the locals had ample opportunity.

Bethlehem was a small village. If Joseph's family had never lived there, and no child named Jesus had been born to his family, every local would have known. If Joseph and Jesus' ancestry had been a lie, the true family of David in Bethlehem would have been the most zealous to disprove it and purify their family line in the eyes of the public. If the massacre of innocents had never happened, every local could dispel the lie.

If you were inventing prophetic fulfillment after the fact, you wouldn't do it this way! You only record such verifiable details for one reason: they really happened this way.

If Jesus had not fulfilled these Bethlehem prophecies, it would be the easiest thing to disprove. But no one could. There's not the first hint historically that anyone denied these events, not even among Jesus' fiercest religious opponents who had all the motive, means, and opportunity to do so.

Jesus fulfilled these prophecies publicly, even as an infant. Anyone could verify them. That's why we're still talking about them.

Third: Many of these fulfillments contain details that no one would want to invent after the fact.

Consider the prophecy for Messiah being born of a virgin, which we discussed in the last chapter. It comes from Isaiah 7:14, which reads:

> "Therefore God Himself will give you a sign: the young woman [*almah*] shall conceive and bear a son, and shall call his name Immanuel [*God with us*]" (Isaiah 7:14, ESV)

The word *almah* always refers to a young woman of unsullied reputation. When a team of faithful Jews translated Isaiah into Greek in the Septuagint, they used the Greek word for "virgin" — because any unmarried *almah* would be a virgin. This was simply how the word was understood, even two hundred years before Mary conceived Jesus.

But there is a small bit of wiggle room: it could be pressed to refer to a young woman on her wedding night.

Thus, if the Gospel writers tried to slip this prophecy in after the fact, you'd expect them to describe Mary conceiving Jesus on her wedding night. It would have fit the definition of *almah* closely enough, and it would have avoided scorn or shame.

Instead, the Gospels record this prophetic fulfillment as a source of unending shame for Mary, Joseph, and Jesus. No one believed Mary's story that she was pregnant by the

Holy Spirit. Even Joseph rejected her story until he experienced an angelic visit of his own.

The public never forgot Mary's shame. Even as an adult, Jesus' enemies threw the shame in His face, accusing Jesus of being the child of fornication (John 8:41).

If Jesus' followers wanted to invent prophetic fulfillments after the fact, for goodness' sake, why would they invent the most shameful fulfillment possible? If they wanted people to revere Jesus and follow Him, why would they invent a story putting Jesus and His mother to unending shame in the public's eye?

There's only one reason the Gospels would record details like this: they really happened this way.

———

How do we know the New Testament writers didn't simply write that Jesus fulfilled the prophecies in the New Testament after reading them in the Old?

Because if Jesus hadn't fulfilled them, no one would follow Him, and we wouldn't be talking about Him.

Because Jesus fulfilled them publicly, even as a baby, making them easy to verify.

Because many of the fulfillments contain details no one would want to include unless they indeed were true.

129

Even as readers coming to these stories millennia after they occurred, we have plenty of reasons to trust that Jesus truly fulfilled ancient prophecies, over and over and over.

This is why prophecy exists: to amaze us, to prove beyond a doubt that the God who prophesied the future is unlike any other religion, any other deity, any other holy book. God makes claims that no one else can make, that no other religion has dared to make in all history:

> "I make known the end from the beginning, from ancient times, what is still to come. I say, 'My purpose will stand, and I will do all that I please.' [...] What I have said, that I will bring about; what I have planned, that I will do." (Isaiah 46:10-11 NIV).

Challenge Twelve:
The Curse of Jeconiah Blocks Jesus from the Throne of David

What if prophecy *blocked* Jesus from being Messiah?

It sounds bizarre, but it's true. Jeremiah the prophet records a declaration from God that blocks David's descendants from the throne, without which Jesus can never be Messiah.

This is one of the seeming impossibilities inherent in the challenge of Messiah's appearing — a challenge no one knew quite how to resolve.

According to prophecy, Messiah *must* be a descendent of David:

> The LORD swore to David a sure oath
>   from which he will not turn back:
> "One of the sons of your body

I will set on your throne." (Psalm 132:11, ESV)

This is an oath that God swore personally to David:

When your days are fulfilled and you lie down with your fathers, I will raise up your offspring after you, who shall come from your body, and I will establish his kingdom. [...] And your house and your kingdom shall be made sure forever before me. Your throne shall be established forever.'" (2 Samuel 7:12-13, 16, ESV).

God's promise could not be more certain: He will surely place a descendent of David on the throne forever.

Yet Jeconiah, one of David's descendants, suffered a terribly specific curse at the time of the Exile. Jeconiah served as the second-to-last king of God's people in Jerusalem. He reigned barely over three months before Babylon conquered Jerusalem to took Jeconiah away into captivity.

God did not bless his reign, but cursed it, as God's people had long fallen into rebellion against Him.

God declared over Jeconiah:

Thus says the LORD: "Write this man down as childless, a man who shall not succeed in his days,

> for none of his seed shall succeed in sitting on the throne of David and ruling again in Judah." (Jeremiah 22:30, ESV).

Jeconiah sired several children, yet God directly blocked any of them (or their descendants) from the throne. This might not be a problem for Messiah; after all, David had many children. Perhaps Messiah could descend from one of them?

Yet Matthew denies that possibility. He opens his Gospel with a genealogy full of surprises:

> The book of the genealogy of Jesus Christ, the son of David, the son of Abraham. [...]
>
> David was the father of Solomon by the wife of Uriah, and Solomon the father of Rehoboam, [...] and Josiah the father of Jechoniah and his brothers, at the time of the deportation to Babylon. [...]
>
> And after the deportation to Babylon: Jechoniah was the father of Shealtiel, and Shealtiel the father of Zerubbabel, [...] and Matthan the father of Jacob, and Jacob the father of Joseph the husband of Mary, of whom Jesus was born, who is called Christ. (Matthew 1:1, 6-7, 11-12, 16 ESV)

Messiah *must* be a descendant of David to be able to rule on his throne.

Yet none of Jeconiah's descendants may ever sit on the throne of David or rule in Jerusalem. God blocked the Davidic line from fulfilling His own prophecy.

And Jesus' claim to the throne of David descends straight from Jeconiah.

How could God ever solve such a puzzle?

Through the virgin birth.

Matthew records Jesus' genealogy through Joseph, Jesus' adoptive father. Joseph descends from Jeconiah through Solomon, giving Joseph legal right to the throne. But as a physical descendent, Joseph is barred by the curse from sitting on the Throne or ruling in Judah. So, too, would any of Joseph's physical children be barred.

So Jesus did not descend from Joseph physically.

Mary also descended from David, but not through Jeconiah. Mary's line ran through Nathan, instead of Solomon:

> Jesus, when he began his ministry, was about thirty years of age, [...] the son of Nathan, the son of David (Luke 3:23, 31, ESV)

This gave Mary royal descent, yet her line did not possess

the legal right to the throne of David. That ran only through Solomon — and Jeconiah.

When the Holy Spirit conceived Jesus in Mary, no male of Jeconiah's line was involved. This avoided his curse, which applied only to his seed — his physical descendants.

Jesus therefore came from untarnished royal blood, a direct descendant of David through Nathan.

Jesus also inherited the legal right to the throne of David as soon as Joseph adopted Him.

Legal rights passed on to the firstborn male, even if that child was adopted, instead of natural born. As soon as Joseph adopted Jesus, the legal right to the throne revived.

Matthew records the precise moment this occurred:

> An angel of the Lord appeared to him in a dream, saying, "Joseph, son of David, do not fear to take Mary as your wife, for that which is conceived in her is from the Holy Spirit. She will bear a son, and you shall call his name Jesus [...] When Joseph woke from sleep, he did as the angel of the Lord commanded him: he took his wife, but knew her not until she had given birth to a son. And he called his name Jesus. (Matthew 1:20-21, 24-25, ESV, emphasis added)

Gabriel gave precise directions: *Joseph* must name the child. Naming a child burst with meaning to the ancient Israelite audience: to adopt a child, you name the child. The moment Joseph gave Jesus His name, Joseph became the legal father of this child.

And Jesus became the legal heir to David's throne.

For generations, the legal right had passed to people unable to wield it. The curse on Jeconiah's seed kept them from the throne. For the first time in centuries, the legal right passed to a descendant of David who bypassed the curse and now could ascend to the throne.

Thirty-three years later, when Jesus ascended to the Temple during the day of the Triumphal Entry, Jesus claimed it as Messiah — the King. David's heir had returned to claim his throne.

Or as Nathanael said,

> "Rabbi, you are the Son of God! You are the King of Israel!" (John 1:49, ESV)

And as even Pilate asked,

> So Pilate asked Jesus, "Are you the king of the Jews?"

"You have said so," Jesus replied. (Luke 23:3, NIV)

Or as we sing every Christmas:

Joy to the world!
The Lord is come.
Let earth receive her King!

Challenge Thirteen:
The Christmas Story Can't Change My Life Today

To much of the world, the Christmas story of Mary, Joseph, and Jesus may be a beautifully written cultural artifact from 2,000 years ago. It may even be true. But question that rise above everything else is this: *what does it matter?*

What it does it mean for me, today? What difference can the Christmas story make in my life, right now?

What difference can the Christmas story make to those who are lonely?

What difference can it make to the poor, the downtrodden, the ones who are always taken advantage of by everyone else?

What difference can the Christmas story make to the oppressed and marginalized?

What difference can it make to those whose lives have fallen apart, who have lost all hope?

What difference can it make to those who feel empty, without purpose, devoid of meaning, like life is one cosmic joke?

What difference can it make to talk about Jesus entering the world?

Let's find out.

―――――

The heart of Christmas is one simple name: Immanuel. Christmas is only Christmas because God is with us. This is a simple idea, expressed in a handful of words. But if it's true ― if God indeed is with us ― then nothing can stay the same.

To examine the difference that makes, we'll follow the wise men through their journey to Jesus. We've covered their story already, in earlier chapters. This time we'll focus not so much on the details of how it happened, but rather the meaning behind it:

> After Jesus was born in Bethlehem of Judea during the reign of King Herod, wise men from the East came to Jerusalem. "Where is the one who has been born King of the Jews?" they asked. "We saw

His star in the East and have come to worship Him." (Matthew 2:1-2, JC:TGL)

What does it mean that God is with us? First of all, it means this: God is speaking. He gives us His Words, filling the Bible with them. He gave the message hundreds of years in advance, through precise, detailed prophecy, so He even writes His message in the skies!

We've explored all these details in past chapters.

But the message to you, right now, is this: *God is speaking to you.*

Our problem is never that God has ceased speaking. God is *always* speaking. God is with us, and He is not silent.

If we want to hear from Him, we have only to open our ears, open our eyes, and ready our hearts. He has already given us His Word.

God's message is universal. He speaks to everyone. The wise men perceived His message, finding it in the stars where anyone could.

Yet God's message is also personal. It captivated the wise men so deeply that they traveled a long and dangerous road to find the newborn King of the Jews.

Their goal was to worship Him — to see who He is, to rejoice in what it meant, and to savor the rich satisfaction it impressed upon their souls. It made the wise men happy to find Jesus. His presence overwhelmed them with a joy unlike any other.

God is *with us*.

God *sees us!*

God *cares about us!*

God took on flesh and lives among us. He is not "too good" for us. He doesn't scorn us. He isn't angry at us.

God is here, with us. He *wants* to be with us.

More to the point: God wants us to be with Him. God wasn't content to stay in Heaven, letting us suffer and falter on earth apart from Him. Jesus took on flesh to live and die for us, opening the door to Heaven, so that we could all be with Him forever.

God is with us — and that is very, *very* good news.

But to some, it was terrifying:

> When Herod heard about this, he grew anxious — and all Jerusalem with him. (Matthew 2:3 JC:TGL).

At the news of Jesus, Herod grew troubled — and rightly so! Herod was brilliant, but brutally wicked. He loved all the trappings of power: he taxed the poor relentlessly, he built excessive monuments to himself, he killed anyone whom he perceived as a threat. Herod lived as evilly as he desired, getting away with it all because he held the power.

And yet now there's a new King, announced in the heavens by God. This is Messiah — the One who ends injustice, the One who brings peace, the One who heals our brokenness, the One who saves us from the terrors no one else can. This new King will set things right.

In the Messiah, God is with us. That means evil always ends. Roman oppression, Nazi Germany, Communist Russia — it doesn't matter how powerful a nation may be. God topples evil empires for breakfast.

This means that all the evil you face will one day die. Its days are numbered. If you follow Jesus — if you live eternally as He bled and died to make possible — then you will outlast all the evil you face. Every evil person, every evil empire, every evil situation, all of it will crumble and fade away, but you will live on.

God is with us. Evil can't survive.

> [Herod] called together all the chief priests and the teachers of the Jewish law and demanded to know where the Messiah was to be born.
>
> "In Bethlehem of Judea," they replied. "For this is what the prophet wrote:

> 'You, Bethlehem in the land of Judah, are certainly
> not the least among the rulers of Judah; for out of
> you will come a ruler who will shepherd my people
> Israel.' (Matthew 2:4-6 JC:TGL).

Who were these chief priests? They claimed to be priests of God, to know the Bible, to represent God, yet they're working with Herod. Why? The answer isn't hard to find: they loved money and power. They conspired with Herod to leech as much money as possible from the common people when they came to worship God at the Temple the priests controlled.

God is with us, and God is speaking. But we must take care. Sometimes, those who claim to represent God care more for the money and power the name of God can bring to them.

This is what happens when you hear some things from God, but not everything. These chief priests loved the verses about coming to the Temple and giving God your money, but they ignored the verses about caring for the poor, ending injustice, taking care of the orphan and the widow, and making sure everyone has food to eat.

This is what happens when we only listen to part of what God says, and ignore the parts we don't like: we end up supporting injustice, we end up supporting government systems that abuse people, we get greedy, and make the name of God a stench to those who need Him most.

143

These chief priests knew the Bible! But they didn't know God. They knew a lot about God, but didn't know Him.

They knew where Jesus would be born. But they don't go. They claim to represent God to the people, whenever money is involved. Yet when God comes down among them, they care nothing about going to see Him.

God is with us.

But if we let the trappings of money and power captivate our hearts, we can find ourselves ignoring Him.

We can know so much about God without ever knowing Him personally. We blind our own eyes every time we cling to sin: greed, pride, selfishness, lust, power, gluttony, hatred. Every sin we choose to cling to divides us forever apart from God — so much so that we wouldn't even go see Him if we knew right where He was.

Christ is Immanuel: God with us. Why did Jesus have to come? Because we love sin. We love money, position, and prominence, like those false priests. We love power, comfort, and selfishness, like Herod. By ourselves, we'll never give them up.

So Jesus took those sins on Himself on the Cross. He died for them, to take them away from us, so that we could be with God. Jesus died so that we could *want* to be with God. Jesus died so that when we have the chance to draw near to God, we go.

> Then Herod sent secretly for the wise men and asked them the exact time when the star had appeared. He then sent them on to Bethlehem. "Go," he said. "Search carefully for the young child. And when you have found Him, bring word back to me. Then I, too, can come and worship Him." (Matthew 2:7-8 JC:TGL).

Like many who crave power, Herod lies. He seeks only to know where the child king lives so that Herod can send soldiers to kill Him.

God is with us.

To some, this is cause for rejoicing.

For others, this is cause for murder.

There are two types of people who seek Jesus: those who seek Jesus for the sake of finding Jesus, and those who seek Jesus for the sake of serving themselves.

Herod wanted to find Jesus because Herod only cared about Herod. He wanted to kill Jesus so that nobody would take away his throne, his money, his power, his comfortable life.

This is a trap every human can fall prey to. If you seek Jesus just to see what He'll give you, if it's all about you and not about Him, then you'll end up just like Herod. When Jesus says something that might threaten your comfort, your money, your life, you'll do away with Him. You'll ignore Him, kill Him from your life. You may even say He doesn't exist, or that He isn't God, because you don't want Him messing up your life. That's the heart of Herod. And Herod's story did not end well.

But if you are like the Wise Men, if you seek Jesus solely to seek Jesus, seeking to know Him, to worship Him, to feel the satisfaction of worshiping the One whom God designed your heart to cherish — that's the abundant life. That is true Christmas joy:

> After hearing the king's instructions, the wise men left. And the star they had seen in the East went ahead of them until it stood over the place where the child was. Seeing the star, the wise men were overcome with joy. (Matthew 2:9-10 JC:TGL).

How often have you been overcome with joy? How much would you give to have that experience again?

This was the greatest joy that the wise men had ever felt. This was the highpoint of their lives.

God is with us. God is speaking, promising things that seem impossible, yet they come true before your own eyes. This means you can trust God, even when He says stuff that seems impossible. He can make even the impossible happen.

146

He can give you the greatest joy, the desire your hearts have always craved, whether you knew it or not. God can give you Himself:

> As they entered the house, they saw the young child with Mary, His mother, and they bowed down and worshiped Him. They opened their treasures and presented Him with gifts: gold and frankincense and myrrh. (Matthew 2:11-12, JC:TGL).

If you seek Jesus, you'll find Him. He *wants* you to find Him. This is why He came; this is why Immanuel, God with us, came to us. He wants you to find Him — and He is not far from you, even now.

And when you see Him, you'll worship. The wise men saw God's impossible promises come true before their eyes; they saw God, the same God who created everything, right there in front of them as a baby.

The same God who created the universe, the same God who created the stars and used them to reveal His coming, the same God who gave us this Bible. This is God, and He is taking on flesh because He wants to be with us. He wants to be with you.

God is with us.

And He loves you.

God knows you're not perfect. He knows life is a mess. It is for all of us. But He still wants to be with you.

Or to put it this way: God knows everything about you, absolutely everything, and He loves you more than you can possibly imagine.

If you find that hard to believe, look at the evidence. This is Immanuel, God with us. He knows the mess we live in. Look at this crazy mess surrounding His birth! He never expected to find a perfect world of perfect people. He knew how dark the world would be. Jesus came because this world needed a Savior.

God is with us. Jesus entered this world joyfully. He came for you — to find you, to love you, to save you, and to welcome you home to be with Him forever.

So let Him. Draw near to Him. Let Jesus be your God. This is where you find life!

This is the meaning of Christmas: God is with you.

Challenge Fourteen:
Christmas Asks Nothing of Me

Without Mary, Christmas could not exist. She is the central heroine of the entire narrative, the one person whose choice determined whether Christmas occurred or failed. Her story is captivating — not only for what happens to her, but for how she responds when everything she knew about life changed.

This simple fact reveals a startling amount about how God works. His heart is to work with us — not to override us, lord over us, or implore us. God hopes to work with us, God and humanity united in purpose to shine light into the darkness.

In this final chapter in the quest for Christmas, let's delve deep into the story of Mary and what it reveals about God.

This may be risky. It may shatter the comfortable distance we've retained between ourselves and Christmas, the neutral peace devoid of expectation where Christmas serves me, but I give it little.

Christmas may yet ask something of you.

But, as it did with Mary, it will give you *far* more in return.

The all-powerful God coming to earth

When Jesus chose to empty Himself and enter the earth, He could have come any number of ways. After all, He is God. He could have come to any people He desired. He could have come any way He desired, to any palace He desired, to any family of wealth and power that He desired.

But Jesus chose to come to Mary and Joseph, two very young people who were possibly still in their teenage years.

Jesus could have forced Himself upon them.

He could have demanded obedience.

Instead, He asked.

It came about in this way:

> In the sixth month, God sent the angel Gabriel to Nazareth, a town in Galilee, to a virgin named Mary. She was engaged to a man named Joseph, a descendant of David. The angel came to Mary and

said, "Greetings, you who are richly blessed! The Lord is with you."

Mary saw him and was troubled by his greeting, wondering what it might mean (Luke 1:26-28, JC:TGL).

Think for a moment what Mary was feeling.

Gabriel sought a private conversation with Mary; no one else is present. Yet in the ancient world, privacy was rare. They likely weren't in a house, as most homes had one large family room which everyone used at the same time. They weren't in the busy village square, as too many people would overhear.

Perhaps Mary was walking in the countryside. Perhaps she found a peaceful shade tree and took a moment to pray. Perhaps she thought she was all alone.

The out of nowhere a voice speaks, startling her: "Greetings, you who are richly blessed!"

Would Mary assume this person was an angel? It all depends on how the angel chose to appear. At sometimes in Scripture, an angel appeared as a normal human; at others, they let their glory radiate out in all their brilliance.

My guess is that Gabriel held back his radiance and appeared to be human. If he had shown brightly, Mary would have little cause to doubt who had sent this messenger. But as it was, "she was troubled by his greeting, wondering what it might mean."

Gabriel must reassure her:

> The angel said, "Don't be afraid, Mary, for you have found favor with God." (Luke 1:29, JC:TGL).

Gabriel needs to reassure Mary: I'm not here to hurt you or take advantage of you. You're safe. I'm here because you have found favor with God.

At these words, Mary could finally see this visitor as an angel, a messenger sent from the Throne of Heaven. As a faithful Jewish girl, Mary grew up studying the stories in the Hebrew Bible. She knew the significance of a messenger from God: everything is about to change.

This reveals one startling aspect to the heart of how God works: when God shows up, He finds us exactly as we are.

Mary isn't in any particularly spiritual place; she's at home in Nazareth, a dirty, peasant village, far away from the Temple of God in Jerusalem. She would have been wearing the standard working clothes she used for doing all her daily chores. She was simply living her life, and into the midst of her day-to-day normality, God suddenly appears.

Mary is given no warning. God does not send her a message, saying "I'm coming to you tomorrow, so clean yourself up, don't do anything wrong today, be especially kind to everyone you meet, and pray a lot. Then, after you've made yourself clean and holy, I'll come to you."

No. The angel appears instantly, right in the midst of Mary's daily routine. She doesn't have to make herself especially holy for God to come to her, as if she is not good enough for God unless she makes a special effort.

She is good enough for God, exactly as she is.

So are you.

God is not waiting for you to clean yourself up or to earn your way to Him. God does not need to pay Him back for the wrong you've done. This is a truth both beautiful and terrifying; God can show up to you at anytime, anywhere, without warning. Even when you feel the least ready and the least worthy, God still wants you, God still sees you, God still loves you, and God still calls you.

> The angel said, "Don't be afraid, Mary, for you have found favor with God. Listen! You will become pregnant and will give birth to a son, whom you are to name Jesus. He will be great and will be called the Son of the Most High. The Lord God will give Him the throne of His ancestor David and He will reign over the descendants of Jacob forever.

> His kingdom will never end."

> "How is this possible," Mary replied, "since I am still a virgin?" (Luke 1:30-34, JC:TGL).

The angel lays out God's plan — and Mary is more confused than ever.

This isn't what she expected. This plan of God didn't make sense; it didn't fit with the way she thought her life would go. She planned to live with Joseph as wife and husband once he made their house ready, raise a family in their small hometown, and enjoy all the daily pleasures of a normal home life. She had matched her vision of life to what everyone around her expected an average, decent life to be like.

But now, her life would be anything but decent. She would be accused of adultery, probably being hated by their morally upright neighbors. Joseph (if he still wanted anything to do with her) might have a hard time finding work, with everyone thinking he and his wife had no regard for the laws of God.

Mary's religious community would have been very proud of her as a young, upstanding woman of God. Yet now they would call her a harlot and ban her from the synagogue for her perceived marital unfaithfulness. Gabriel mentions great promises, and an incredibly grand picture of who their son would be, but the road to those grand times would be painfully bumpy.

God's plan would change everything. This was a plan so grand, so life-changing, so epic, that Mary couldn't fathom how it was physically possible.

Gabriel answered her question, not deterred in the slightest:

> "The Holy Spirit will come upon you, and the power of the Most High will overshadow you. And so, the Holy One born to you will be called the Son of God."
>
> "And listen! Elisabeth, your relative, has conceived a son, even in her old age. She is already in her sixth month—she who was said to be unable to bear children! For with God, nothing is impossible." (Luke 1:35-37 JC:TGL).

Gabriel answer's Mary's question — then leaves her with a choice.

God designed a plan for Mary, one completely unique to her, a plan so unexpected it seems impossible and so life-altering it feels overwhelming.

But Gabriel bathed this plan in a promise: Nothing is impossible with God. An elderly woman like Elizabeth, long past the age of childbearing, can conceive and carry a child.

Gabriel presents God's plan, promised and proven possible.

Then he leaves Mary with a choice.

We don't know how long Mary pondered her options. She may have responded immediately. Or Gabriel may have waited, patiently allowing Mary time to watch competing futures flash in front of her eyes.

Then Mary makes her decision:

> "I am the servant of the Lord," Mary replied. "May what you have said truly happen to me."
>
> Then the angel left her. (Luke 1:38 JC:TGL).

Mary runs immediately to spend time with Elisabeth. She witnesses the impossible conception made possible, the baby John leaping in his elderly mother's womb as soon as Mary appears. Mary hears Gabriel's promise echoing in her ears: Nothing is impossible with God.

A few months later Mary returns to Nazareth, visibly pregnant. Joseph plans to divorce her until Gabriel appears again, revealing to him everything God planned. Joseph is equally stunned, but he obeys. He responds with the same attitude Mary expressed so well: "I am the servant of the Lord. May what you have said truly happen to me."

Mary and Joseph had a unique situation and a unique story to live out. Never again will Jesus appear in flesh through a virgin birth.

Yet the way God worked in Mary and Joseph's lives reveals how He works in each of us.

God showed up dramatically, altering their entire lives.

Yet what He asked of them was remarkably simple. He didn't ask them to achieve great things, or to be superbly moral people. What God wanted was simply a willing heart. God only wanted them to trust Him.

Consider how daunting their task was. These two young, inexperienced, overwhelmed teenagers would be responsible for caring for and raising the most important baby ever born. You would think that God would send an army to protect this child, that Jesus would be guarded by soldiers, kept behind thick walls in a palace or fortress, with preachers at every doorway, making sure people knew the importance of this child.

Yet in reality, God only need faithfulness. If Mary and Joseph would obey, God would supply everything else.

God brought shepherds from the field to see the child, to sing of His coming, to celebrate with this young family about their amazing birth. God brought visitors from the east, wise men of wealth to provide financially, giving this young family incredible gifts of frankincense, myrrh, and solid gold. God provided constant divine guidance and protection, telling them how to avoid everyone who wanted to cause them harm.

Mary and Joseph chose to trust God.

And God took care of everything else.

———

As we celebrate this Christmas season, the time when Jesus came to us, know this with all certainty: this is how Jesus comes to you.

The message of Christmas is not that God comes to you with a huge list of expectations and demands, and that you must perform well or perish. That's not Christmas. The message of Christmas is not that you need to clean yourself up, that you need to work your way to God. That's not Christmas, not in the slightest.

The message of Christmas is that Jesus is fully willing to come into your life right now, exactly as it is, whether it's messy or imperfect or boring or hectic or whatever else it may be. He doesn't care that your life isn't perfect. He cares about *you*. He wants to be with you, to be near to you, to let you know how much He loves you.

God wants to be with you. It's who Jesus is, expressed so powerfully in His name: He is Immanuel. He is the God who yearns to be with us.

Jesus comes to you right now, exactly as you are. This is the message of Christmas, the one aspect that sets this holiday apart from all others: God is coming to you.

And He has a question for you: Will you trust Him? Will you let Him be God not only of the entire universe, but also of your life?

The reason for Christmas, the reason Jesus needed to come to earth, is that God has always wanted to be with us, but humanity keeps rebelling against that plan. We want to be the gods of our own lives. Rather than let God be our God, rather than let Him mess up our lives with plans we don't even understand, we want to stay in charge. Rather than love and trust God, we love other things, and we trust in other things to make us happy. We trust that we can make ourselves happy if we only get just what we want.

But it never works, not for long, not the way we hoped. We rebel against God because we seek anything and everything else above Him. We all have sinned. We all have fallen short of His joy, of His glory, of the peace He showers to those on whom His favor rests.

We all rebel against God, and for that, we all deserve to die. No country on earth tolerates rebels. If you sell out your country and violate the commands of its king, it gives you the death penalty. God is far more than a country. God is the Author of life. God *is* life. And if you rebel against life, you get death.

Yet God demonstrates His own love toward us in that while we were still sinners, Christ died for us. Jesus came into the world at Christmas not to condemn the world, but to *save* the world through Himself.

We rebelled against life itself, and so someone had to die. We had to die! But God wants to be with us. God wants us to live. So Jesus took our place. He took our death, He died on our Cross, so that in His death our rebellion would end, and we would be free to dwell with God forever.

And for this to happen, for us to enjoy this incredible gift, all we need are willing hearts. God does not demand that we earn this. He only demands that we accept it, that we choose Him as our personal God, that we are willing to trust Him and follow Him in all He calls us to do, just as Mary and Joseph did.

When the angel showed up to Mary and Joseph, he spoke the words of God over them, and gave them a choice. They responded by saying, "I am the servant of the Lord. May what you have said truly happen to me."

God extends this same chance to you, right now. Christmas is no mere holiday. Christmas is a choice, the chance for

160

you to seize the destiny God planned for you from before your beginning — or to let it pass by.

Christmas asks you to make a choice. It asks you to partner with God, to accept His plan for you, to let Him work through you to shine His light into a dark and lonely world.

Mary and Joseph said yes. Because they did, Light itself filled the world, the Author of Life born to defeat death. Because they said yes,

> "The light shines in the darkness, and the darkness has not overcome it" (John 1:5, ESV).

God has light for you to shine into the world. There is light that you alone can shine, work that you alone can do, people that you alone can love.

God wants to work with you to shine. And if God shines His light in you and through you, the darkness will flee. Jesus is the Light Himself. Darkness cannot overcome Him. Jesus is light and life, and He wants to fill you to overflowing.

Hear the words of God spoken over you, and if you choose, respond to them as Mary and Joseph did. These are the words that Jesus says to you, right now:

"You were dead in your sins and rebellion, but I love you more than you will ever be able to imagine. I love you, and your failures and dark spots won't keep me away. I went to the Cross for you. I took

all your pain, all your failures, all the hidden scars you hide from the world, and I suffered them for you. They're gone, if you will accept my gift of deliverance from them. I will deliver you from these sins and fill you with a new heart, with a new spirit, with new life. I have great things planned for you, things you can't imagine right now. If you will let me be your God, if you will believe that I died for you and came back to life, then I will give you new life."

These are the words that Jesus speaks over you. If you want this, this amazing Christmas gift, all you have to do is respond in your heart: "I am the servant of the Lord. May what you have said truly happen to me."

May this be for you an exceedingly merry Christmas. May the Light shine.

Endnotes

[1] Oberdier, Carl. Personal conversation on Quora.com. 20 November 2021.

[2] Ehrman, Bart. "Why Was Jesus Born of a Virgin in Matthew and Luke?" *The Bart Ehrman Blog: The History & Literature of Early Christianity*. 24 December 2014, https://ehrmanblog.org/why-was-jesus-born-of-a-virgin-in-matthew-and-luke/

[3] Ibid.

[4] Skobac, Michael. "Jews and Christmas: a Bad Match." *The Canadian Jewish News*. 7 January 2016, https://jewsforjudaism.org/knowledge/articles/jews-christmas-bad-match

[5] Krakowsky, Susan. Personal conversation on Quora.com. 16 November 2021.

[6] Brown, Raymond Edward. *An Adult Christ at Christmas: Essays on the Three Biblical Christmas Stories*. Liturgical Press, 1978, 17.

[7] Brown, 17.

[8] Martin, Ernest. "The Nativity and Herod's Death." *Chronos, Kairos, Christos: Nativity and Chronological Studies Presented to Jack Finegan*. Edited by Yamauchi, Edwin. Eisenbrauns, 1989, 89-90.

[9] Strabo, *Geography* 12.6.5; Tacitus, *Annals* 3.48.

[10] Tacitus, *Annals* 1.11, emphasis added.

[11] Hoehner, Harold W. (2010-06-29). *Chronological Aspects of the Life of Christ* (Kindle Locations 105-124). Zondervan. Kindle Edition. Emphasis added.

[12] Roman Census Edict in Egypt (Papyrus 904). Cited in Deissmann, G.A. *Light from the Ancient East*, 2nd ed. Hodder and Stoughton, 1910, 268-69.

[13] Oberdier, Carl. Personal conversation on Quora.com. 5 December 2021.

[14] Bailey, Kenneth. "The Manger and the Inn." *The Presbyterian Outlook.* 21 December 2006, https://pres-outlook.org/2006/12/the-manger-and-the-inn-a-middle-eastern-view-of-the-birth-story-of-jesus/

[15] Dickman, Laurel. "Christmas Isn't Christian: The Pagan Roots of the Winter Holiday." *Wear Your Voice Magazine.* 2 December 2016, https://www.wearyourvoicemag.com/christmas-pagan-roots-winter-holiday/

[16] "Old Christmas Day." *Encyclopedia of Christmas and New Year\'s Celebrations, 2nd ed.* 2003. Omnigraphics, Inc. 20 December 2021 https://encyclopedia2.thefreedictionary.com/Old+Christmas+Day

[17] "The unexpected origins of popular Christmas traditions." *CBS News.* 25 December 2018, https://www.cbsnews.com/news/the-unexpected-pagan-origins-of-popular-christmas-traditions/

[18] Magness, Jodi (2021). *Masada: From Jewish Revolt to Modern Myth.* Princeton University Press. p. 126.

[19] Macrobius, *Saturnalia*, 2:4:11.

[20] Josephus, *Anitiquities* 17.6 174-175.

[21] Bair, Kyle Davison. "Who Wrote the Books of Matthew, Mark, Luke, and John?" Quora.com. 19 May 2020, https://www.quora.com/Who-wrote-the-books-of-Matthew-Mark-Luke-and-John/answer/Kyle-Davison-Bair

[22] Lüdemann, Gerd. Virgin Birth? *The Real Story of Mary and Her Son Jesus.* United Kingdom, Bloomsbury Academic, 1998., 140.

[23] Sweeney, Marvin Alan. *Isaiah 1-39: With an Introduction to Prophetic Literature.* United Kingdom, William B. Eerdmans Publishing Company, 1996. 161-162.

Made in the USA
Middletown, DE
27 November 2022

15796099R00099